The Prosperity Approach:

The Simple Formula to

Ultimate Prosperity

By Allyson Chavez

Acknowledgments

To those whom a mere 'thank you' can never suffice, I attempt to do so anyway:

Justin Jepsen: my colleague and fabulous friend. Thank you for your expertise in book writing, your helpful critique and deep conversations. You were the glue that kept me together. Thank you!

Heather Godfrey: my amazing editor. You managed to get me to dig deeper and pull things out of myself I didn't know were there. What a gift!

My book launch team and early readers: Thank you for your honest feedback and incredible support through the book launch process. There is no way I could have done this without you!

Jeremy, Jeryson, Branson, Trevin and Peyton: Living with a wife and mother who is on a mission can't be the easiest thing in the world, and yet you always stand beside me, support me, comfort me and believe in me. You are my angel team! God must really love me, to give Jeremy to me as my spouse and to let me be the mom of such incredible children.

Heavenly Father and Jesus Christ: I never thought I had anything to say, let alone write in a book. You gave me the words to say and write, and the circumstances necessary to experience Ultimate Prosperity. You have taught me of your reality and love in ways that are too deep to adequately express. Thank you for this mission and the means to accomplish it. And thank you for picking up all the slack that this weak human being leaves in her wake. You make all the difference!

Table of Contents

Chapter 1
Are We There Yet?

————————•————————

Prosperity is a way of living and thinking, and not just money or things. Poverty is a way of living and thinking, and not just a lack of money or things.

—Eric Butterworth

What is prosperity, anyway? Is it a number in your bank account, a certain neighborhood you live in, being able to do whatever you want whenever you want to do it? How do you know once you've "arrived"?

The dictionary defines prosperity as "a successful, flourishing, or thriving condition, especially in financial respects; good fortune." (Dictionary.com)

But I've experienced the dictionary's definition of prosperity, and although on one level I definitely fit the "mold" of prosperity—making high six figures, vacationing in Hawaii with my family multiple times a year, buying our dream cars—but on a much deeper level I didn't feel very prosperous at all. I woke up in anxiety and fear almost every night, only it was fear that I wouldn't be able to sustain this level of living. I was terrified I would lose it all.

Since that wake-up call I've created my own definition of true prosperity: *true prosperity* is a level of living that is not governed by fear or lack.

In Catherine Ponder's book, *Open Your Mind to Prosperity,* she says that, "You are prosperous to the extent that you experience peace, health and plenty in the world."

To me, *true* prosperity goes far beyond how much is in your bank account. It's having the energy to do what you'd like to do in a day; it's a deep connection with the people you love best in this world, and being able to effectively communicate with everyone who comes into your sphere of influence. It's feeling great in your skin; and it's having enough money to be able to experience those things in life that enhance your soul.

Maybe your soul would be enhanced by driving a sporty new car or living in an elegant home. If it is, wonderful! Embrace it! My soul is enhanced by beautiful views of nature, exotic locations to make memories with my family and husband, experiencing culture, and enjoying others' talents in art, theater and music. Those experiences require a degree of prosperity to be able to enjoy them.

With nearly a decade of working with clients and doing research on my own, I've discovered three things that keep most people from receiving the level of prosperity they want:

1. They're unaware of the role energetic frequency plays.
2. They violate universal laws of creation because they don't know what they are.
3. They have subconscious programming that they're not even aware of, which holds them back from the life they desire.

Solid Foundation

For years I've studied how to build prosperity. I've come to realize that a solid foundation is critical if you want to create true, lasting prosperity, which I know you do simply because you're reading this book. And when you can apply a simple prosperity formula on a regular basis, prosperity is inevitable.

The Prosperity Approach: The Simple Formula to Massive Prosperity is the most straightforward approach to prosperity I could create. The formula is this: **3 Pillars + 2 Secrets = 1 Prosperous Life.** And when you learn and apply this formula, it leads to prosperity every single time.

This book is not meant to spout theory. This book will cover the secrets, pillars and strategies to create real, lasting prosperity. The exercises are meant to be done while you're waiting in line at the grocery store or sitting in traffic, they're meant to be assimilated into your daily life. There are some activities that will require you to carve out some time if you want to do them correctly, but you'll enjoy the processes and will look forward to the next thing to do!

Why should you listen to me, anyway?

My name is Allyson Chavez. My last name is pronounced CHAV-iss. It rhymes with Travis. I'm a regular person, just like you. I'm a prosperity coach specializing in the inner work that's required to create true, lasting prosperity. I'm also a certified SimplyHealed ™ energy practitioner, a licensed and certified BANK ™ sales and communications trainer, a speaker and an author. I started my online business in 2012 and built it to high six figures in just over two years. It was the hardest thing I've ever done professionally in my life. Prosperity thinking did not come naturally to me when I started out.

I grew up in a home that taught survival and scarcity, rather than thriving and prosperity. Perhaps you can relate to that. My mom had severe depression, back when very little was known about mental illness. It's my belief that it started as post-partum depression when my twin brothers were born when I was eight. This was in the mid-80s, when post-partum was called "baby blues." But due to severe financial strain my parents were under when the twins were born, the depression quickly spiraled into much more than baby blues. It got so bad that I never knew what I was coming home to after school. Usually it was to see my mom in bed watching *Eight is Enough* and working on a cross stitch. Or she'd meet my older sister and me at the door and leave as soon as we got home to go to therapy sessions. We'd be in charge of our four younger brothers until she or my dad arrived home later that evening. I was nine at the time and didn't understand what was going on; I just knew that my family wasn't a happy one, and something was very, very wrong.

When I was eleven my mom committed suicide, leaving my dad alone to raise six children ranging in ages from thirteen to three year old twins, along with paying staggering medical bills and mountains of debt. It's no wonder I lived in survival—that's exactly what my dad was doing, trying to keep his family together.

I decided in high school that I would live a life different from my parents, like just about every other teenager in the world. I wanted to live in confidence and wealth, have a safe family where everyone felt loved and supported, and an environment where money was plentiful and stress was low.

Fast forward twenty years. I was married to an amazing man, had four incredible children of my own, and a successful business in direct sales. I'd created that safe environment for my kids that I'd never had as a child, but money certainly didn't flow, and stress certainly wasn't low. And even though I was successful, I was bored and unhappy in my business but terrified to try something different.

I felt whisperings and a pull toward the industry of energy healing, but knew nothing about it and was terrified to move forward for fear of making a mistake, being deceived spiritually, wasting money, and putting my family in dire straits financially.

As a woman who is both spiritual *and* religious, this industry of "energy healing" was scary because it could get so "woo woo" and mystical very quickly. In fact, one of the only fights my husband and I have ever had was due to my interest in energy work. As I was getting more interested, he got more skeptical. Since it was so new to me, I couldn't articulate it very well, which increased his skepticism and made him that much more convinced I was being deceived. The more I pushed, the more he pushed back. Though we were at an impasse, I didn't want to sacrifice my marriage. So, for four years I ignored my growing interest, and we didn't speak of energy work at all.

But the whisperings of my heart got louder, the pull got stronger, and my discontent became more pronounced.

Enter the "dark night of the soul." Because of my own experience, I believe that if there is a different, higher path you're to walk, God will start with whispers and nudges, and if you don't listen He'll raise the volume and add tugging, and if you're still not getting the message, life gets massively uncomfortable, until it reaches the point where the pain of staying the same is greater than the pain of change. That's what He did with me.

The most difficult year of my adult life was 2011. My husband and I wanted to move into a better area to raise our children, but because of the housing market crash a few years before, our house and land were devalued and a deal we were almost ready to close on came crashing down around us. We were devastated to be stuck in a neighborhood we didn't like with no viable options to make our conditions better. Ten days later, on Easter morning, my brother Tyler died in his sleep. He was thirty years old, had been married for three weeks, and had no money. He lived three hundred miles away, so the family all traveled and pooled our money together to help pay for his funeral. I remember donating $500, which was a third of our savings, figuring God would bless us because we were being generous and serving.

The week after his funeral, my husband's car engine died, requiring a new engine that took every bit of our savings, leaving us with literally *twenty-eight cents* in our bank account. Three days later, our oven caught on fire. Thankfully, no one was hurt and no damage occurred to our home, but we had no way to pay for it because we had no credit cards, having worked really hard previously to get out of debt, and I was devastated at being abandoned by God.

My faith had always been my bedrock, but now it was shaken to its core. Here we were, doing our best, serving and donating money we didn't have to support my brother's new widow and pay for his funeral, and what does God do? Turn His back on me. I felt that He knew exactly what was going on in my life and just didn't care. That was more devastating to me than not believing in a God at all.

I did everything I could think of to connect with Him: I read the scriptures, went to church faithfully every week, prayed, and felt . . . nothing. Not one ounce of support, comfort or love. I remember praying one night, asking for a hug. That's all I wanted. I was desperate to know that heaven cared and was close by. That night I dreamed that not only had my mom and my brother died, but my dad died, and I was left completely alone in the world.

That was the proverbial straw that broke me. I was doing everything I could think of to do, and my God wouldn't even throw me a little scrap of comfort when I so desperately needed it. So I turned my back on Him. I stopped praying, stopped reading the scriptures, and would have stopped going to church except that I still had faith in my religion, and it was important to me that my children have a strong spiritual foundation and grounding.

For several months I became cynical and snarky, which wasn't like me at all. The world got darker and darker, until one day a small voice reminded me about energy work and the universal law of attraction, and I was making this experience harder and darker than it needed to be, regardless of my relationship with God.

I began looking for what I called "pinpricks of light" in my dark, abysmal world. Instead of focusing so much on how everything was falling apart, I began to actively look for things that made me feel a little bit better. For example, I had a core group of girlfriends I'd known since elementary school, and they rallied around me and showered me with love. My marriage was still strong, in spite of the financial strain we were under. And if I had to lose a family member, I was grateful it was my adult brother who I had a great relationship with; there were no regrets. In spite of my grief I knew it could have been so much worse—I didn't lose my spouse or a child.

As I swung my focus from all that was wrong and instead started looking for things that were right, I began to feel a tiny bit of relief. I followed that small light, and as I did I noticed that people began to come across my path, energy workers and thought leaders, and I felt hopeful in a way I hadn't felt in at least a year.

I began to study universal laws and was reminded that my thoughts were influencing my experience which made it harder, darker and last longer than it needed to. Gradually, I realized that feeling abandoned by God was due to my own blocks, and my own beliefs about not being supported. Once I realized that, I began to pray again, trusting little by little and following the whispers of my heart. I began researching different energy modalities online, just to see what was out there. And I began to open myself up to receive spiritual guidance in different ways from before.

We were able to sell our home very quickly in early 2012, even though it was at the bottom of the market and we knew it. But for once, there was something more important than money, and I was happy to take a small amount of equity and move, even though there wasn't another home to move to yet. In the meantime, my family of six moved into the 2 bedroom basement of my husband's parents' home while we went house hunting.

It ended up being a wonderful arrangement, because during this time I finally began feeling supported again. Since we only had a small rent payment to make, we actually had money left over every month! For the first time in our lives my family took a big vacation, and we went to Disneyland. I started feeling safe where money was concerned, and learned more about universal laws and how they work in my life.

Through a series of remarkable "coincidences", I began to make plans to phase out of my direct selling business and I was led in a very divine way to practice energy work, which had the most profound impact on my life up to that time. I became intimately acquainted with my intuition, and I *just knew* that I needed to share this new life with others, that it needed to be created as a business, and it needed to be done online.

And I had absolutely no idea how to do it.

For the first time in my life, I let go of the hows and trusted they'd be shown to me as I went. I focused on the next things to do, which was to set up a website and get certified in this new modality. It took six months to do that. During this time I knew I'd need a business coach, so I was actively looking for one online. As I continued to move my feet, God continued to direct my steps. I was led to the coach I needed at the time, and she taught me how to take a practically nonexistent business to six figures in a relatively short amount of time. It took me about two years to grow my business to that level, and within a few short months, it grew again.

Looking back at that dark, bleak time of my life, I'm filled with wonder, awe and gratitude that it happened. Though I wouldn't want to revisit it, that experience is what led me directly to this work I do that makes my heart sing every day. Life as I know it today would not have been possible without the devastation experienced in 2011. The deep darkness is what opened the way to inconceivable light, which is what inevitably happens when you look for the light.

The Prosperity Approach: The Simple Formula to Massive Prosperity

Believe me, my friend. I've been there. I know the fears, the anxiety, the wonderings and the constant mind chatter along the road to prosperity. I've experienced first-hand going from nothing to something bigger than I'd ever managed, back to nothing again. (More on that later.) Through this journey, I've learned the things that work and the things that distract. I've learned how simple it is to create prosperity, with the full understanding that simple does not mean easy. By using the pillars and secrets I have discovered along the way, I've changed every aspect of my life for the better.

We live on a planet that operates in linear time. This means that there is a time buffer with everything we experience. The time buffer varies in length, some things take seconds, while other things take years, but the time requirement is there. It will take some time to create true prosperity. It doesn't have to take a really long time, so take heart! However, if you want true prosperity to last, you'll have to skip the magic bullet. It requires patience, consistency, persistence and dogged determination. But it's the best way you can spend your time, because not only is it a ton of fun, but you'll be spending it learning the *true* process of creation.

This is your handbook to prosperity. By using the strategies taught in this book, you'll be able to shortcut your way to prosperity. Through a lot of trial and error, and prayer and inspiration, I discovered the 3-2-1- Formula for True Prosperity: 3 Pillars + 2 Secrets = 1 prosperous life.

This is the book I wish I'd had when I first started out!

How to use this book

I don't believe in only teaching the theory of prosperous living. I'll give you the theory and the philosophy, but I'm more interested in the *practical application* of the philosophy of prosperity. You can understand prosperity on an intellectual level, but if you don't feel it in your core, you'll never experience it to the degree you want.

You'll notice that this book is laid out like a workbook. This is, after all, your handbook to prosperity. So use it! You'll find tips and exercises that will assist you in connecting to the feeling of prosperity in a very short amount of time, which is crucial when you're deliberately creating a prosperous life.

Be sure to stop and do each exercise before moving on to the rest of the book. You'll also notice space for you to jot down impressions. If you want to get the most out of this book, you'll do everything this book says. It will lead directly to prosperity. Keep a highlighter handy and mark passages that are important to you. That way you can easily flip open this book and see what grabbed you, and you can use those passages as reminders of what to focus on every day.

Creating true prosperity is fun! It doesn't need to be a chore! In fact, if it feels like a chore, you can bet that you're actually pushing prosperity away from you. So, take a light- hearted approach to this book, and don't take yourself so darn seriously.

Chapter 2
The Two Secrets to Prosperity

———————•———————

"I came upon one of the most ancient and universal truths—that to affirm and claim God's help even before it is given, is to receive it. Desire, Ask, Believe, Receive."
-Stella Terrill Mann

Why am I starting the explanation of the formula with the secrets instead of the pillars? Because, as you'll soon learn, this formula is dependent on the secrets. Effectively creating true prosperity revolves around the two secrets, but the formula would be really confusing if it was 2-3-1, wouldn't it?

Prosperity, at its core, requires only two things. That's it. And while on the surface they look quite simple, they're much harder to execute in reality. True prosperity is dependent on knowing and mastering these two secrets, because everything turns on them.

I remember when these secrets first came to me. I had created a high income, but because of my inner frequency and undisciplined thoughts, I lost that income within a year of creating it.

I'd built my online mentoring business around teaching universal laws as a way to create miracles in your own life. I loved teaching and mentoring! But I didn't have the correct mindset or skill set to effectively enroll more clients into my program, and I didn't hold my value. I began to worry that I might be charging too much. I wondered that if my clients didn't see results, was that my fault? And as I allowed those thoughts to take root, it led to greater self-doubt and fear that I would lose everything I had worked so hard to build.

I'd also attracted quite a few entrepreneurs who wanted me to mentor them privately, to show them how to grow their businesses as quickly and as successfully as I did mine. I figured that since I'd done it,

I could teach it! And while that is technically true, it's like eating a plate full of brownies: just because you *can* doesn't mean you *should*. Teaching business building was not my genius or passion, and I stepped out of alignment with my purpose by taking on private clients and teaching them business strategies. That added to the pressure I heaped on myself because now I was *really* worried what would happen if my private clients didn't get results or a return on the significant investment they had made with me.

As a result of not holding my value, staying true to my purpose and being disciplined in my mindset I had a harder time enrolling clients, and I didn't even want to renew the private clients I did have because I was so afraid I would "fail them." So clients weren't renewing, and I wasn't signing on new clients to work with, no matter how I tried to "skill up" in sales. The truth was I'd build my company on pure energy and grit, and I was burned out and didn't even realize it. As you'll learn later on in this book, the principles worked perfectly, so *by law* the money had to leave.

We were now "broke at a higher level." Life was tempting me to go to another dark place, but I refused to give into that temptation again. I remembered the lessons I had learned four years before: my thoughts had made that dark time last longer and harder to get through than it needed to be. I was going to do it differently this time.

I had invested a lot of money into higher learning and personal development after we hit that income, but none of that education had brought a return on my investment yet. As I watched our income go down as our expenses went up, panic really wanted to settle in. I desired to unlock the secret to prosperity, but my mind kept shrieking at me to throw in the towel and get a "real job" somewhere else, even if was $10 an hour.

God ended up having a stern talking with me one afternoon, which became the turning point in my prosperity. I was going back and forth in my mind about moving forward and figuring this out, or going back to trading time for dollars and doing energy work for my own benefit. My attitude was pretty defeatist, and I remember the thought suddenly coming into my mind asking what I was going to do. Was I going to get up again and again and again until I figured this out, even if it took the next fifty years? Or was I going to give up, give in, and get a "nine to fiver", without ever reaching my goal? It was my choice, but the choice needed to be made. I didn't feel judgment either way, God would love me regardless of what I chose. I knew that each choice would lead me in a vastly different direction. That's when I declared to myself and to God that I was in this for the long haul. I'd stick with it as long as it took to master the inner work of prosperity.

God commits

Now

> *"Until one is committed, there is a hesitancy, the chance to draw back—concerning all acts of initiative (and creation), there is one elementary truth that ignorance of which kills countless ideas and splendid plans: that the moment one definitely commits oneself, then Providence moves too. All sorts of things occur to help one that would never otherwise have occurred. A whole stream of events issues from the decision, raising in one's favor all manner of unforeseen incidents and meetings and material assistance, which no man could have dreamed would have come his way. Whatever you can do or dream you can do, begin it. Boldness has genius, power, and magic in it. Begin it now."* –William Hutchinson Murray, from his 1951 book *The Scottish Himalayan Expedition.*

That's when things began to change. My outer circumstances hadn't changed yet, but I had changed on the inside, and that's all that was required.

I think what I Become

Connect to God Learn How to Receive

Change my MIND

THINK & Grow RICH

> "In order to change external circumstances, you must change the cause. Most men try to change conditions and circumstances by focusing on conditions and circumstances. To remove . . . lack and limitation, you must remove the cause, and the cause is the way you are using your conscious mind."
> —Joseph Murphy

I knew that a massive change inside me was all that was required to create an eventual massive change in my circumstances. So I celebrated the change going on within me and concentrated on holding that new inner state as long as I could, as often as I could. Because that was the key.

I was in my office one day, pondering on prosperity and what it really takes to create it, when this thought came to me as clearly as one man talking to another: "Allyson, you only have two jobs: connect to Me, and learn how to receive. That's it. Everything else will take care of itself." I knew right then that those were the two secrets to prosperity: connecting to God and receiving His gifts. The inspiration about the pillars came a little later, as physical, practical ways to support us as we connect and receive.

So let's unlock those secrets a little more, shall we?

Prosperity Secret #1

The first secret to true prosperity is connecting to your True Source. Most of us confuse *channels* of prosperity and the *source* of our prosperity. Our bank account, job, businesses and bosses are not our source of prosperity, they're simply different channels which God uses to bless you with financial abundance. And if your spiritual language isn't God or Heavenly Father like mine is, just substitute whatever vocabulary resonates most with *you* to describe your Higher Power.

Too often we connect to our job and our bank account and rely on those to bring us prosperity. When the job changes or is taken from us, we immediately worry and fear that our prosperity has been cut off. We rely on ourselves and our own genius to get us out of financial trouble, and though we pray, our faith can feel weak and feeble, especially if we're consumed with fear and doubt.

Connecting with your True Source of prosperity changes everything! Understanding that the job doesn't provide you with money, that God is your Source for everything good in your life, automatically increases your faith and trust as you turn to Him for guidance, comfort and assurance.

Most people feel like they have a good connection with their Higher Power. But it's *maintaining* that connection that can get a little tricky. It's crucial to be able to hold that connection—no matter what is going on—for prosperity to come more easily into your life. How often do distractions get in the way of staying connected to God? In my own life, I know that meaningful prayer and scripture study can be very difficult to maintain on a daily basis. And yet, I also know how important they are to grow a relationship and strengthen my connection to my Source.

"If Satan can't make you bad, he'll make you busy." –Adrian Rogers

---

I looked up "connecting" in the dictionary. It reads: "to join together so as to provide access and communication." (dictionary.com)

As I read about "connecting" in context to my relationship with my Higher Power, it suddenly gave new meaning to the whole word, and *why* I want to connect with Him. I realized it's so that I can gain access to Him, and then communicate with Him! We relate to what we can connect to, and having continual access and clear communication will blast the lid off your prosperity.

It gave such an interesting spin on why daily prayer or meditation and scripture study or another form of spiritual, uplifting study are so important. We access our Higher Power when we put our mind and thoughts on a spiritual plane, and He communicates with us through the scriptures and other spiritual writings. These two things assist us in connecting us to a God who loves us more than we can imagine and who wants us to experience prosperity more than we even want it for ourselves.

How to connect with our True Source of prosperity

Albert Einstein said, "When the solution is simple, God is answering." As human beings we tend to over-complicate things so much and then dismiss the simple answers as something we'll try "later." But it really is very simple to connect to God. That doesn't mean it's always easy, but it can be done in a matter of seconds and the effects can be long lasting.

The first thing to do when connecting to God is to decide that the universe in which you live is a friendly one.

I love Albert Einstein. You'll see me quote him throughout this entire book. He said, "The most important decision you'll ever make is if you live in a friendly universe or a hostile one." Whether you agree with that or not, it's still a thought worthy to ponder. Spend some time with that idea and then decide where you stand. God created everything that is, including the planet and the universe. Did He create it to be friendly to our desires, or hostile? The decision you make concerning that one fact influences every other decision you'll make. It determines whether you pursue your dreams with boldness or timidity; it dictates whether you take inspired risks, and it especially influences your relationship with God.

My thoughts about my Higher Power have changed quite drastically throughout the years. We tend to picture God much like we picture our earthly fathers, and that can work for us or against us. In my case, it worked against me.

My father is a wonderful person. However, we have never been close in our relationship. Praise and outward affection didn't come often when I was growing up, and so I pictured God as this arms-crossed, "I'll help you if I feel like it but don't count on it" kind of Deity. So often we've heard the word "No" from our fathers or other male authority figures, without any other explanation or justification.

I remember as a child, whenever I'd ask my parents for something, I'd literally close my eyes and wait for the worst, because I expected a no but I didn't want to see it coming. And that's how I approached God in prayer. Many times my parents wanted me to defend my position about *why* I wanted what I was asking for, silently requiring me to prove that I deserved it and show what effort I was willing to put into getting it. So when I'd pray for something I really wanted, like prosperity, I'd go to prayer with a list of reasons about why I deserved it, how I would prove my worthiness to receive it, and then I'd beg for His help *but not really expect to get it.* I'd metaphorically reach my hand up to try to grasp His, but then talk myself out of it and tell myself I'd go to God once I'd figured it out on my own.

That's not a very effective way to connect with God.

So, when I first started learning the art of connecting with my Higher Power, instead of picturing this disapproving, frowning Man just daring me to make Him do anything, I simply pictured the universe we live in, and how everything works together so smoothly. I'd picture the staggering abundance nature provides on this planet, and the laws that govern the blessings we receive.

The universe that God created isn't a being, it's just one of His creations. It functions based on immutable, unchangeable laws. The laws work the same for a "bad" person as a "good" person; they don't play favorites. I can be the nicest person in the world, but if I step off a building the law of gravity is going to pull me down regardless.

We live in a universe of order. There are laws that govern physics, math, and every other science. When you obey those laws, your experiments work. There are also laws that govern thought and creation. When you obey these laws, your experiments work! If I want to create the life of my dreams, I simply need to obey the universal laws that govern creation. This helps me want something without feeling the need to justify why I want it, or checking to see if I deserve it, or asking someone else's permission to have it. If I want to launch a rocket into space I don't need to beg an invisible Being for permission to do it. I need to study and know the laws of math and physics, design the rocket in my mind, engineer it on paper (or in a computer program) and then into an actual rocket, make sure the environment is conducive to a successful launch, and then launch it! It's the same with realizing our dreams, or creating physical prosperity. The universe is impartial. And that helped me to claim what I wanted without fear or embarrassment. If it seems a little fuzzy right now, hang in there! It will get clearer as we go.

Ultimately, knowing that God created the universe and everything that is in it for our growth and enjoyment helped me to connect with Him in a deeper, more meaningful way.

I've included a list of different ways you can connect with your Higher Power. This is by no means comprehensive. In fact, I invite you to add to this list with your own ways that you connect to Him!

1. **First and foremost, assume that you're not alone, and that God does want to be part of achieving your dreams.**

I liken this to "assuming the sale." Having been an entrepreneur for nearly two decades and taken numerous sales and marketing classes, I've been taught to "assume the sale." That is, assume that the potential client *wants* what you're offering and will happily pay you for it. So, assume that you're not alone in this venture into true prosperity. Assume that God is right beside you and is anxious to assist you in achieving your goals. Expect God to support you along the way! And expect that support to come from various delightful channels.

It's crucial to effectively connect with your True Source to have the belief that this Source wants what you want. Now, right around this time is when a lot of people bring up the question of God's will vs. their will. If it feels right in your heart, brings value to the world, and harms no one (including yourself), walk confidently in that direction. God will assist you in course correcting as you go. The desire to create prosperity was placed there by Him, after all. Something that helped me when I first started was to tell God that I was going in this direction because it felt good in my heart, right in my mind, and expansive to my soul—even when it also felt a bit scary, and that if I was headed down the wrong path, to stop me. More than once, He *has* stopped me before I've gotten too far down a path that wasn't right for me and my life's purpose.

I love this quote by Edwene Gaines, "Having directed faith means having a heart-felt specific desire, coupled with a deep and abiding trust in the goodness and generosity of God, and therein lies that magic and power of setting our goals."

Assuming that you're not alone and that your Heavenly Father is by your side as you learn to create prosperity is another way of describing "directed faith." This faith will shock you with how quickly you feel connected to God!

2. Prayer

Don't read this as a pat Sunday School answer. And if you're not religious, that's okay! Whether you're religious or not, it's vital that you connect to your Higher Power, or the God of your understanding. The best way to do this is through prayer. When you learn how to pray correctly, this is the most powerful tool to connect you to God. How do you pray correctly? In my experience, I know that when I *listen more than I speak*, I feel more connected. Have you ever had a conversation with someone and you can't get a word in edgewise? It leaves you wondering if you're even a necessary component in this conversation at all!

I had a friend many years ago who only needed an open phone line to have conversations that were hours long. All the input I was required to contribute was an occasional "Mmm hmmm" and "oh really?" And there was more than one occasion when I would set the phone down and mute it, and walk away from the conversation for a few seconds, because I wasn't needed to keep the conversation going.

Remember, connecting is about joining together for access and communication. In order for communication to be effective, there must be giving and receiving. If your mind is filled with chatter, fear, worry, anxiety or anger, there is no room to be able to receive communication from Him during prayer. Work to quiet your mind before praying, and picture what you do want instead of what you currently have, then ask God if He'll help you to achieve what you *want,* instead of saving you from whatever perceived crisis is going on in the moment. Then go still and listen. $10K per month

You might get an answer, or you might not. If no answer is coming, picture God standing next to you, giving you strength and love. "Pretend" if you must at first. Let it all be okay, no matter what is going on.

Some of the deepest, most connecting prayers I've ever had have been when I've said very little.

3. Walking on the grass in bare feet

I know this sounds a little "out there", but have you ever tried it? If you haven't, take off your shoes and socks, take this book outside with you, and go walk on the grass for five minutes!

There are many health benefits from walking on the grass, soil, or sand in your bare feet. This is also called "earthing." It stimulates nerve endings in your feet which are connected with various organs in your body, being outside in the fresh air rejuvenates your senses, vitamin D from the sun is absorbed in your body, and all of this actually serves to soothe and relax your body and your spirit.

I love to lie down on the grass and then focus on where I can feel the grass beneath me. It's easiest for me to feel the grass on my fingertips and hands. Then I focus on my sense of smell and breathe in the grass and other scents around me. I'll engage my ears and listen for the birds and other noises, and eventually I'll open my eyes to search the sky and look at the clouds, the trees and the evidence exploding in nature that God is real, and He has created a world of abundance for us to enjoy!

4. Acknowledgement

Proverbs 3:5-6 says, "Trust in the Lord with all thy heart, and lean not unto thine own understanding. In all thy ways acknowledge Him, and He shall direct thy paths."

One of the reasons life got so hard and dark for me back in 2011 was due to the fact that I wasn't acknowledging God for the good in my life. In fact, I was blaming Him for the bad!

To acknowledge something is to recognize its existence or accept it. To me this means in every way we can think of, see God there. See Him in every situation, good or bad. Because He is there, in every situation. When you can see God in the rebellious child, or the car accident, or the late bill, as well as in the budding flower, the promotion and raise, and the miracle of recovery, it makes your connection to Him unconditional. It makes the good times last longer and taste even sweeter, and shortens the bad times and makes them smoother to navigate.

5. Gratitude

Gratitude is one of the simplest, most profound ways to connect to God that I've ever experienced. I had a good friend give me a plaque that says, "Gratitude turns what we have into enough." That plaque sits right on my desk, where I can see it all day long.

Gratitude is all about being thankful, expressing appreciation and kindness. Gratitude isn't contingent upon how things are going in life. In fact, when you can find things to be grateful for during those rough storms in life, it actually helps to calm those stormy seas and leads to smoother sailing.

I've heard the quote, "Envy is counting someone else's blessings." Gratitude is all about counting and *feeling* your own blessings. It's not just the big things we express gratitude for, the small ones carry just as much weight as the big ones. In fact, they might carry more.

I make it a practice to express gratitude out loud for small things as well as big things. I love saying thank you for green lights, beautiful weather, a soft pillow, small sales in my business, hugs from my kids, drivers who let me in, close parking spaces, discounts, and so forth. The "small" things generally get as much enthusiasm as the "big" things, like book contracts, signing high level clients, hugs from my teenage son (that definitely qualifies as a big thing!), raises, fabulous vacations, my marriage and children, my health, and so forth.

Writing it down is a powerful way to anchor gratitude directly into your heart. Pen to paper connects head to heart and requires you to reflect on those things that are working in your life, regardless of all the things that don't feel like they're working right now. If you don't have a gratitude journal, I suggest you get one. A notebook or random scrap of paper will do to start. Before going to bed, list three things you're grateful for that happened that day. Sometimes I've written that I'm grateful the day is over and I get to go to bed! As you start to express gratitude more and more often, you'll find more and more things to be grateful for. And more things to be grateful for will be brought to you. Busy your mind with gratitude and wonders will begin to happen in your life.

It's Gratitude Time!

Take a moment to list five small things you're grateful for, as well as five big things you're grateful for:

Starting the process of Wayne out of my life –
Bl 61 Wings @

6. Quiet times of reflection

"Be still, and know that I am God." (Psalms 46:10) This scripture has become a mantra for me, especially when I'm feeling frantic, or if I'm connecting more to fear and scarcity than I am to God and prosperity.

In today's ridiculously paced world, we've allowed for very few times of quiet reflection. Yet it's those times when we're quiet that are the best times for us to connect to our Higher Power. When our mind isn't swirling with to-do lists and worries and constant mind chatter, we're so much more receptive to feeling Spirit.

Is this hard to do? Well, it can certainly feel challenging. I believe things are as hard as you make them, though. It can be tough to start, for sure, but starting will create that connection you seek. And it's okay to start small. Confucius said, "The man who moves a mountain begins by carrying away small stones."

7. Meditation and Visualization

Before you get nervous that I'm going to have you sit in the lotus position and say 'ohm' for a half hour, allow me to share with you what my meditation practice looks like. When I first started, I set the timer for three minutes. During those three minutes, the goal was simply to quiet my mind. I never tried to clear my mind; I just wanted to quiet it. So, as a thought would come, I would gently remind myself to let it go. When another thought would come in I'd acknowledge it and let it go. By "let it go" I mean I wouldn't concentrate or focus on that thought anymore. It was a very refreshing way to spend three minutes! I think I'm up to five minutes now. And that's plenty of time for me. It's another small yet powerful way to connect to God.

Another wonderful way to connect to my Higher Power is by visualization. I learned this from Marianne Williamson and have had amazing experiences through it. Close your eyes and see your body infused with light. Imagine that every cell is filled with a golden elixir that God has poured into you. Picture angels gathered around you as you let go of everything and focus on connecting with the light and love God has for you. Hold the image for five minutes, breathing out your burdens and breathing in the miraculous power of God's love. See light pouring into your body. Use this visualization when any problem occurs to you.

8. Awareness of coincidences

Einstein said, "Coincidence is God's way of remaining anonymous." (I told you I love Einstein!) All those little serendipitous things are really God at work in your life, but He works subtly, and if we're not tuned in, we'll miss or dismiss it as a coincidence.

For example: When I was having a really hard time, and fear and anxiety were my constant companions, it seemed that every time I got in the car and turned on the radio, "Home" by Phillip Phillips would be on. And it would inevitably be playing, *"Settle down, it'll all be clear. Don't pay no mind to the demons they fill you with fear. The trouble it might get you down. If you get lost you can always be found. Just know you're not alone. 'Cause I'm gonna make this place your home."* (Holden & Pearson (2012). Home, (recorded by Phillip Phillips), On *The World from the Side of the Moon*, Interscope 2012)

At the time I remember wishing those words were meant just for me. Yet, they were! Every single time! Especially because I don't listen to the radio or music very often when I'm driving, I prefer the silence. But I'd feel like having some music in the car, and it would be that song, over and over and over again. Those "coincidences" are God connecting with you. But that connection is dependent on your awareness of what it truly is.

Nancy Thayer said, "(God) is always speaking to us . . . sending us little messages, causing coincidences and serendipities, reminding us to stop, to look around, to believe in something else, something more."

9. Spending Time in Nature

Whenever you hit the beach, or go the mountains, or experience some form of nature, does it seem that your soul just breathes a sigh of relief? My belief is that this happens because Heavenly Father created the planet, and He also created us as his crowning achievement. So being in nature is a perfect way for us to "touch God" for a little while.

I love sitting on the beach, which only happens a few times a year because I live in a land-locked state. I love watching the waves crash, looking out over this vast body of water that no man could ever make. I especially love watching the sun set over the ocean. It's breathtaking. It's so easy for me to connect to God at that time. I feel so big in that moment, like I can do anything! God designed *all* things to benefit and uplift His children. And of all the wondrous things He created, *I am His crowning achievement!* If He takes care of the sparrow that has fallen from the tree, *of course* He's going to be with me to help me succeed. I feel that most strongly when I'm surrounded by His abundance in nature.

10. Scripture Study or reading spiritually uplifting literature

My favorite way to study the scriptures is what my friend Carolyn Cooper calls the "pick and roll." Ask a question, pick up the scriptures and roll it open to a random page, and start reading until you find the passage that jumps out at you. I've had more spiritual experiences and felt such a strong connection to God when I've read scriptures this way than by any other way. And I've also realized that there isn't anything "random" about the page I've happened to open to!

If the Bible or other books of scripture aren't your bag of tea, choose writings by someone you admire and respect that are uplifting and help you feel connected to your Higher Power.

As I said before, this short list of ways to connect to God is by no means comprehensive. In fact, you probably have your own ways to connect to Spirit that I didn't mention. So, write those things down in the space provided below. This will give you easy reference when you come back through this book again.

_____

_____

_____

_____

_____

_____

_____

_____

Okay, I've connected. Now what?

You've got half of the equation down! But remember, you don't connect once and then you're done. The trick is a constant connection to God—or as constant as you can manage here in this human form on earth.

To form this constant connection, you must have a conscious awareness of when you're connected and realize when you've disconnected. Hint: if you're feeling fear or anxiety you've disconnected from your True Source of prosperity. When you're disconnected, you then get to make that conscious effort to reconnect or stay connected to Him. And sometimes you're reconnecting many times in a single day. But as you practice and stay committed to being connected to your True Source of prosperity, you'll find that connecting gets easier and you stay connected for longer stretches of time.

Are you ready for Secret Number Two? Then keep reading!

Prosperity Secret Number Two

You think that only connecting to God is enough to experience prosperity? It's not. Have you ever known someone really spiritual, really connected to God, but they're broke? Or their relationships are in the toilet? That tells me that being connected is the first step, but it's not the only step.

You must also learn how to *receive*. Everything turns on receiving.

Okay, back to the dictionary! To receive means: "to experience, to take into one's possession, to be given or presented with; to be paid; to detect, to admit, acquire."

Did you catch the first meaning? *To receive means to experience!* So, if you're not experiencing prosperity in some form in your life, you're not receiving it.

What do you receive—or experience—every day? Do you experience stress? Worry? Fear? Doubt? Do you experience frustration? Do you experience exhilaration or peace? How about abundance and contentment? What do you mostly feel and mostly think about during the day? That will give you a clue as to what you receive on a very basic, energetic level. (We'll get into the energetics later.) Be really honest here. This exercise can be very eye opening. List the dominant thoughts and emotions you experience each day, both positive and negative.

_____

_____

_____

_____

Receiving is oftentimes compared to a radio antenna. When a radio or television receives transmitted signals, it picks them up and converts them into sound or pictures. As human beings we actually do the same thing. We are literal receivers. Information is presented to us by the world, and then we pick it up and convert it into sound or pictures in our own minds. Information is neither good nor bad; it just is. But our *perception* of the information presented to us puts the "good" and "bad" labels on the information, and we create stories and beliefs around that information that directly affect whether we'll receive more of what we want, or more of what we don't want.

For example, several years ago my family moved in with my husband's parents while we were looking for another home to buy. My mother-in-law, whom I love dearly, had a habit of letting the kids eat candy right before dinner. I asked her not to feed the kids candy before dinner, to which she agreed. But when my five-year-old asked her for candy, she replied, "I can't give you any. Your mom said I can't give you candy ever again."

Now, is that what I had said? Not even close! I asked her not to feed the kids candy before dinner. That was the only restriction I had put on candy. But my mother-in-law took the information I gave her, *please don't feed the kids candy before dinner,* and created a story and belief around that information, *don't ever let the kids have candy again,* which affected her experience.

We do this all the time. The trick is to give it a meaning or a label that will assist us in moving forward, rather than a meaning that holds us back or works against us.

In order to receive or experience all the abundance or prosperity that our Higher Power fully intends for us to receive, we must put ourselves in a position to where we *can* receive those wonderful experiences. There are specific things we do to open us up to receiving, and things that close us down. You might be surprised at how simple and easy it actually is to open yourself up to receiving all the good that life has to offer. It's simply a matter of turning up your awareness and making a decision to receive.

Note: In order to *receive* positive experiences, negative emotion must be let go of *first*. This is very important to know when you're growing into prosperity.

How to open yourself up to receiving more good in life:

1. Smiling

   The act of smiling activates neural pathways in your brain that send a calming message to your nervous system and relaxes your facial muscles. It also releases chemicals like serotonin and endorphins that assist you in feeling better.

2. Laughing and giggling

   According to the Mayo Clinic, laughing stimulates your heart, lungs and muscles, increases your intake of oxygen-rich air, and increases the endorphins released in your brain. It may also lower blood pressure and improve your immune system. (mayoclinic.org) I've found laughter to be a fabulous stress reliever. When I laugh hard enough, it's a great workout for my abs as well!

3. Gratitude

    In my experience, this one deserves a place right in the top 3 of how to receive. As you acknowledge and express gratitude for the blessings you already have in life, you literally place yourself in a position to receive more.

4. Playfulness and fun

    Albert Einstein's son Hans said of his father, "Whenever he felt that he had come to the end of the road or into a difficult situation in his work, he would take refuge in music, and that would usually resolve all his difficulties (Ronald W. Clark, 1971. *"Einstein. The Life and Times"*) Googleplex, the corporate headquarters of Google, is famous for its beach volleyball courts and massive dinosaur skeleton with pink flamingos on it, to assist its employees in fostering creativity by being relaxed and playful. At Pixar, its animators work in wooden huts and decorated caves. When we regularly make time for playfulness and fun, it naturally opens us to receive inspiration, ideas and direction.

5. Prayer or meditation

    Since this is one of the greatest ways to connect with God, it stands to reason that prayer or meditation is also a wonderful practice to open you up to receiving. Quieting your mind and listening makes room for different ideas or impressions to come, because you've created space to receive them.

6. Reading something spiritual

    When you read the scriptures or other spiritual books looking for a specific answer, because you've set the intention of what you want to experience in the scriptures, many times you'll find yourself receiving the answer!

7. Being around those you love.

8. Humility

    When you approach everything as a student, you receive so much more! One of my friends once told me that she believes in learning something from every experience, whether it's easy or rough. She's one of the most upbeat, prosperous women I know!

9. Kindness

    Showing kindness no matter the situation puts us right in the path of receiving wonderful outcomes.

10. Obedience

    All blessings are based on specific commandments and laws. As we obey God's commandments and the laws that govern prosperity, we open ourselves right up to receiving those blessings.

11. Action

    As long as your feet are moving, God can work with you! It's impossible to steer a parked car, so start moving your feet. Even if you don't know what to do, just do something. When your heart is open, even if the action you're taking is the wrong action, God will steer you back on course pretty quickly.

12. Trust

    Trust is "a firm belief in the reliability, truth, ability or strength of someone or something." (dictionary.com) Having trust is a powerful quality that opens you up to receiving more. As you trust that your Higher Power knows exactly what's going on in your life, and that He loves you and makes sure that everything works for your good, it gives you the confidence to try things you've never tried, which opens you up to receive more wisdom, more prosperity and more good. "Counting on God" is trusting Him. When I first started my company and had no idea what to do, I knew that God knew what to do, even if I didn't. I trusted that He would show me as I needed to know. That helped me to move my feet. Trust doesn't happen behind a desk, though. It happens as you practice it.

13. Being generous

Back when we were broke many years ago, the one thing that really opened me up to more prosperity was this adage: "I can afford to be generous." It didn't matter to what degree I could be generous, I *always* had enough to be generous. Sometimes it was a dollar left in the tip jar, for no other reason than I was proving that I could afford to be generous! That simple act, done consistently, increased my ability to receive more money, greater trust in God, and more faith in the unseen. It's a powerful exercise.

14. Giving compliments

Sincerely complimenting someone is acknowledgment of receiving something that benefitted you in some way—whether it's a performance of some kind, or complimenting their smile or a job well done—and it opens you up to receive more goodness in your own life.

15. Finding the gift in every circumstance

This is a powerful way to receive, and also one of the more difficult ways. But when you start looking for and finding the gifts in the hard times, you receive peace of mind, you receive relief, and the hard time literally passes a lot faster.

16. Slow down

A simple task, yet it's not very easy for most of us to do. Give yourself permission to slow down on a regular basis, and watch how your ability to receive increases.

17. Celebrating

A great way to open yourself up to receiving more good is by celebrating the small victories every single day. When my children were young, I used to celebrate when I got a shower before the end of the day. And I remember HUGE celebrations during potty training time! Small victories lead to greater victories, and those bigger victories come faster when we celebrate the small ones along the way.

Okay, now it's your turn!

List a few ways you can open yourself to receive that are not already included in the list above.

_____

_____

_____

_____

Now for a little extra credit:

To assist you in opening up to receive more, please list three victories you've already experienced today, large or small.

    1._____

    2._____

    3._____

Just as there are simple ways we open ourselves to receiving, there are also simple ways we use to block ourselves from receiving. It's important to list what some of those are, so you can be aware when you're blocking and then quickly counteract that with one of the above exercises to open yourself back up to receiving.

How to Block Yourself from Receiving

    1. Fear

Concentrating on fear, or the anticipation of pain, quickly shuts us down to possibilities and prosperity. Fear can quickly consume us. When that happens, say good-bye to receiving what you want. It will shut you down faster than anything else but doubt.

2. Doubt
3. Bad, grumpy moods
4. Being easily offended
5. Holding grudges

   This absorbs so much time and attention, and literally blocks you from receiving more goodness and prosperity. That's why forgiveness has nothing to do with the other person and everything to do with you and your ability to move forward into greater prosperity.

6. Over-reacting
7. Being "in your head"

   If you're spinning in your head and listening to the mindless chatter that goes on all day, you don't have any room to receive guidance or anything that will assist you in moving forward.

8. Not recognizing the blessings that already exist in your life, even during the hard times.

9. Complaining, eye rolling, back biting
10. Apathy
11. Being judgmental of yourself or others
12. Complaining about your situation

    This blinds you to the blessings that are literally found in your situation, and cultivates a sense of entitlement

13. Indifference toward your Higher Power

    Many times this blocks the light that surrounds us and shuts us down to higher levels of inspiration.

14. Ignoring the good that's already there

    This looks a lot like, "Yeah, but…" Have you ever said that to someone who wants you to look on the bright side, or had someone say that to you when you were trying to help them? It immediately blocks you from receiving.

15. Hurry, worry, or rushing

    If we're too busy and filled with worry, there is no room for us to receive good. We're already filled up.

16. Skepticism

    Have you ever tried to explain something to someone and you could tell they didn't want to believe you? When we have the attitude of "*make* me believe" it's a sure shot that we won't believe, and we won't receive.

In what ways do you block yourself from receiving?

Again, it's important to know how you block yourself, so you can catch yourself when you do it and then open yourself to receiving. List ways you block, and stay away from judging yourself on this!

_____

_____

_____

_____

So, now that we've shed the light on ways to open yourself and block yourself from receiving, it's time to dive into *how*. How do you receive prosperity in all its forms on a consistent basis

How to receive

Let go of negative emotions

This must be done first, before you can receive or experience prosperity. Has someone tried to cheer you up before, but you didn't really *want* to be cheered up? Be honest! Of course this has happened to you. Cheering up didn't happen, did it? It didn't until you let go of the negative emotions first.

Ask

This is a very important part of receiving, especially in regard to staying consistently connected with God. Infinite Intelligence wants you to ask for help! He wants you to ask for the prosperity you want. He wants to be your partner, or co-creator in the prosperity story of your life. Ask Him to help you stay open to receiving. You will be delighted at the ways God assists you in your desires.

Believe

As important as it is to ask, we must believe that He will help us receive that prosperity we want. Remember, skepticism shuts us down to receiving more good in life, so believing that you *will* receive is a critical piece to receiving. It's also admittedly one of the most difficult things to do, especially if your world feels like it's crumbling around you and all evidence is pointing to disaster and that things will never get better. But by law, they have to get better. You'll see why in a later chapter when we discuss the fascinating and exciting universal laws of creation. No matter what is going on, you always have the choice to believe. I learned this from one of my mentors: when I have a choice, I choose to believe!

Know what it is you want

You can't have a *general* idea of what you want and expect to get *specific* results. You must know what it is you want so you can be clear in the asking. Wallace Wattles says, "If you send out vague longings you'll get vague results." Also, if you don't know what it is you want you won't know if it's come or not! If you'll sit down quietly and really think about it, you'll know exactly what it is you want. Most of us cloud over what we want because we're afraid to be disappointed if it doesn't come.

Have a soft, open heart

To me, having a soft and open heart looks like being a student at all times, and finding the beautiful lessons that exist in every experience. It's looking for the nuggets of inspiration in every class you take, both spiritual and secular, that help you move forward, instead of expecting to be blown away by new information all the time. It's a willingness to be taught, and a willingness to be wrong.

Prayer or meditation

Praying and meditating correctly requires time to be able to move out of the chatter of your mind and connect to the quietness in your heart. Create a space to receive direction through prayer by praying *before* you're ready to pass out from exhaustion. This is how I often pray: I picture what I want in my mind, to feel what it would be like to experience it, and with that thought in mind, go to God in prayer and ask if I can have it. This is so effective because I'm using my imagination in the way God intended me to: to create the life I desire! Instead of picturing and feeling the disaster waiting to happen and begging God to help me avoid it, I picture the situation I want to have and use my imagination to serve me, asking for heaven's help to bring this or something even better to me. It's a powerful way to pray. Try it sometime!

Keep the commandments

Whether you believe in the Bible or not, obeying the Ten Commandments is a wonderful way to bring peace, happiness and prosperity into your life. God has also created a number of laws, outside of scriptural ones, that lead to prosperity. In fact, in my years of research, I've found over twenty-one universal laws of creation and four mental laws that have been enormously helpful in creating prosperity in my life. Those will be discussed in detail in later chapters. The reason why it's so important to keep all the commandments and universal laws is that God has set up His "rewards system" based on obedience to these laws. That's how God can be an impersonal, unchangeable God, who doesn't play favorites. You obey the law, you get the blessing. You don't obey the law, you don't get the blessing. Simple as that.

Pay attention

"I explain that now, when someone asks me why I cry so often, I say, 'For the same reason I laugh so often—it's because I'm paying attention.'" –Glencon Doyle Melton.

How many times have you "checked out" in your mind and then someone says something funny, and you missed it? I've done that more times than I can count. In order to experience or receive you must pay attention!

Be humble and teachable

Harv Eker says the most dangerous words in the world are, "I know that." I'm sure that many of the things you're reading in this book, you already know. If you find yourself saying, "I know that" throughout this book, be aware of that. You only *truly* know something *when you're living it*. You might know it intellectually, but unless you're experiencing and living it, you don't really know it. You'll know you're humble and teachable when things you've heard before hit you from a different angle and land deeper. You'll feel them anchor more deeply into your soul than they did before.

For years I resisted taking a course on mastering mindset because I was already teaching how to master mindset! What could I possibly learn about a topic I'd already spent years teaching? I finally broke down and took the course because I couldn't get it out of my mind. That course became the most valuable course I've ever taken. I learned things that I'd never even considered before, and it opened up my world in ways I'd never imagined. Powerful, magical things happen when you're humble and teachable about *everything*.

Now it's your turn again!

List some of the how's to receiving. What have you done in the past to open yourself up to experiencing prosperity?

_____

_____

_____

_____

We've discussed the two secrets in The Prosperity Approach formula. Now let's dive into the three pillars that assist us in connecting and receiving!

Chapter 3
Energetic: The First Pillar of Prosperity

———————•———————

"If you want to find the secrets of the universe, think in terms of energy, frequency and vibration"

—Nikola Tesla

Einstein said, "Everything is energy and that's all there is to it. Match the frequency of the reality you want and you cannot help but get that reality. It can be no other way. This is not philosophy. This is physics."

Quantum physics has proven that the essence of absolutely everything in this universe is *energy*. Everything is energy! Break it down small enough and you'll find that the physical make-up of everything on this planet, animate or inanimate, is energy. I am energy, and you are energy. And everything vibrates at a specific frequency. The life you desire has its own specific frequency, just as the life you're currently living has a specific frequency. We live in a universe that is based on energetic attraction. We attract to us people, events and circumstances that match our inner energetic frequency. That's why you get along so well with your friends, and oftentimes have the same kind of experiences in life. You're on the same frequency. It makes no difference if we like the circumstances we're in, on the level of *frequency* we're a match.

James Allen wrote a wonderful book in the early 1900s called *As a Man Thinketh*. He said in that book, "The outer conditions of a man's life will always be found to be harmoniously related to his inner state, both that which he wants, and that which he secretly fears . . . Men do not attract that which they want, but that which they are."

We live in a universe of attraction, and we attract our circumstances on the level of energetic vibration. Have you ever been around someone you feel uncomfortable with? Maybe they're too darn negative and always live in drama, or everything goes their way and life seems so easy for them. The people that are in your life are an energetic match to exactly where you are. "Birds of a feather flock together," is a universal truth. And it has nothing to do with things you have in common and everything to do with where your inner frequency resonates. You might want prosperity intellectually, but if you don't resonate with it on an *energetic* level, you'll never get it. Or you'll get it but you won't be able to keep it because you can't sustain the vibration.

Imagine turning on a radio to a particular station. If you want to listen to classic rock, you must tune into the station of classic rock. That station has a specific frequency, and your radio must match for you to experience it. Even if you're a tiny bit off, you'll simply get static. You might wish or even throw a tantrum that 100.3 doesn't play the music you like that is on 100.7, but 100.3 will not change the music. You must tune into 100.7 to experience what is on *that* frequency.

True prosperity is the same way. You must go to the level or frequency on which it resonates. It can't tune into you.

So, how does all this vibration and energetic frequency translate into real life experience with prosperity?

According to the National Endowment for Financial Education, 70% of those who win the lottery actually go bankrupt within the first five years, and most people say they were more miserable *after* they won the lottery than they were before! (see Time.com "Here's How Winning the Lottery Makes you Miserable.") And though many articles talk about relatives coming out of the woodwork and giving too much money away, the real reason people couldn't hold the money was that they were not an energetic match for that amount of money. If you're not a match for something, you will do everything you can to get it out of your experience, without even realizing that's what you're doing.

I thought I could handle the large amounts of money we suddenly had through my online business. I was wrong. Because I wasn't a match to it on a vibrational level, I was filled with anxiety all the time. I began worrying that my clients wouldn't think I was worth the amount they were investing to work with me. Doubt filled me. I doubted my ability to sustain it, to get more clients, or to retain the clients I did have. And I spent and spent, without saving any of it. Why? Simply because my inner frequency wasn't a match to the frequency of that much money. It truly is that simple.

It's also very simple to detect where your inner frequency is at any given time. It's crucial to know this, since we create our reality based on the energetic frequency we emit. So, if we're going to deliberately create true prosperity—which is the smartest, fastest way to create it— we need to know where we're vibrating at any given time and then change that vibration if the frequency we're in is not a match for what we want.

Emotions are very powerful indicators of where we're vibrating at any given moment. In other words, feelings are signals. Most people don't want to feel their emotions, fearful that they'll be consumed by them. But they're enormously helpful in creating prosperity! As we'll discuss in depth later on in this book, emotions are caused by thoughts. Every emotion you have can be traced back to a thought.

Have you noticed that when you wake up sad or angry, things tend to go wrong all day long? You tell everyone you knew it was going to be a bad day because of how you woke up, and you were right! You were late to work, you had to deal with angry clients or customers, you spilled something on you, everything seemed to go wrong. The reason why everything went wrong is simply because you were a match to the circumstances, people, and events that perpetuated that frequency. And because God has set up this planet and His universe to be one of abundance, more things kept going wrong because you are abundant in your ability to attract.

"Abundance" doesn't necessarily mean good. It just means a large amount of something. There are a lot of people who have an abundance of lack. And sometimes we've created an abundance of things going wrong. However, this is all within your power to change, when you realize what a powerful magnet you are, that you create your life on the level of vibration, and that by changing your thoughts which

> *The energy of the mind is the essence of life.*
>
> *--Aristotle*

change your emotions, you will literally change your reality.

The role the body plays in creating true prosperity

Our bodies are magnificent, miraculous creations! And they also play a very important role in creating the prosperity we want, because our bodies can tell what we translate as truth in our belief system. And we create according to our beliefs, which feed our thoughts, which become actions, which turn into results. Our bodies tell us what is true for us and what is not true for us, and we can feel how energy and vibration move through our body. What's more, when we have the proper tools we can measure it at any time to know exactly where we're vibrating, if there are any weaknesses or blocks in our energy, and where we're strong or weak.

It's called applied kinesiology, or muscle testing.

Within and surrounding the body is an electrical grid, which is pure energy. Because energy runs through the muscles in your body, if anything is introduced to your grid that isn't a vibrational match to it, your muscles will virtually "short circuit" or weaken temporarily. Things that might have an impact on your electrical system are thoughts and emotions, foods, and other substances. If something is introduced to your grid that is a match in frequency, your muscles will stay strong because the energetic circuit wasn't broken.

Using your muscles, we can find what thoughts or beliefs weaken or strengthen your body. If you make a statement that you perceive to be true, your electrical system will continue to flow and the circuits remain strong, allowing your muscles to retain strength. If you make a statement that is false, your energy system will temporarily short circuit and your muscles will quickly weaken or lock up.

The easiest way to feel a physical reaction to energetic frequency is to use the "sway test" on yourself.

Exercise: The Sway Test

Stand up and plant your feet about hip width apart, so you're comfortable standing there. Next, put your hands over your heart. It doesn't matter which hand is on top, just put your hands over your heart. Close your eyes, take a deep breath and think to yourself, "My body loves to drink paint thinner."

Your body loves to communicate with you, and it won't lie to you! Our minds lie to us all day long, but our body and our vibration doesn't. So, think about drinking paint thinner, and notice what happens in your body. Within a second or two, you will begin to sway backward. The direction your body moves is very important: we move forward into our truth, even if that truth doesn't serve us, like believing that there is never enough, and we back away from things that are not our truth. Swaying backward indicates you've introduced something into your energy field that is not an energetic match to what your truth is. You've caused a weakness in your field which has affected your muscles to temporarily weaken, which moves you backwards.

Now take a breath and think to yourself, "My body loves to drink clean, clear water." Give it a second and see what your body does. It will involuntarily move forward. You've just introduced a thought that is an energetic match, and your body moved toward its truth.

Isn't this so cool? Let's test some other things. Make a note of whether you go forward or backward. Use T if the statement is true for you energetically (your body moved forward), and F if the statement was false energetically, or if your body moved backward.

_____ My name is _____. (Use your actual name. You'll go forward.)

_____ My name is _____. (Use a name that isn't yours. You'll go backward.)

_____ I deserve to live my dreams.

_____ I am enough.

_____ I am living my purpose.

_____ I love my job.

_____ I love my life.

_____ I am worthy and deserving of prosperity in my life.

_____ I must work hard to earn money.

_____ I can only make barely enough to cover my needs.

_____ I feel guilty when spending money on myself.

_____ Money comes to me easily.

_____ Prosperity is a struggle.

_____ I am moving forward in my life.

_____ It's easy to be prosperous.

_____ I am confident in creating my dreams.

_____ I live in lack.

_____ I live in prosperity.

_____ It's my birthright to have all my needs met.

_____ It's safe to ask for what I want.

_____ Everything always works out for me.

_____ I'm safe when I am visible.

_____ I am always divinely guided and protected.

_____ My body is healthy and strong.

_____ I'm safe no matter what happens.

_____ I make decisions based on what I think might go wrong.

_____ I make decisions based on what I think might go right.

The hardest part about muscle testing is trusting the answers we're getting. Use statements rather than questions, close your eyes to help get out of your head, and write down whether the statement was true or false for you. If you feel like your body is going all wonky, take a deep breath and tap firmly on your breastbone five times. That will clear your energy and reset you. Then test again.

Sometimes we'll muscle test and be surprised that our energy moved backward when intellectually we felt the statement to be a truth for us. Remember, we can think something all day long, but if we're not a match to it in our inner frequency, we won't reach it. We've got to be an *energetic* match, not just a *mental* match.

Just for fun: If you're feeling frustrated that you can't really feel the energy, close your eyes, put your hands over your heart and think, "Hitler." You'll be amazed at how quickly your body responds to *that* vibration!

Other things you can muscle test on: if a particular food or supplement is good for your body, what vitamins or minerals your body needs, if you need more sleep, more water, what your subconscious beliefs are, even what dollar amount you are energetically comfortable making. Can you think of other things to muscle test on?

Your body and your energy respond to what's true for you, whether or not you're consciously aware of what the truth is. Muscle testing is all about physically connecting to *energetic frequency*, and then distinguishing whether or not *your* frequency is a match to what you're testing on.

A word of caution: muscle testing is only used to test where you are right in this moment, or where you were in the past on an energetic level. It doesn't work for "fortune telling" or future events. Sometimes people are tempted to muscle test if the person they're dating is "The One" or if they'll lose fifty pounds on this particular diet. It's also not to be substituted for decision making. Muscle testing is a tool that tells you where you're vibrating in that moment, and if the vibration of what you're testing is a match to your current truth or not.

Now it's your turn!

Think of some statements you'd like to muscle test on. Write them below and put T if it's true for you, and F if it's false for you.

1.

2.

3.

4.

5.

"Like the sun, the inner Self is always shining, but because of negative clouds, we do not experience it. It is not necessary to program oneself with the truth; it is only necessary to remove that which is false. The removal of the clouds from the sky to illuminate the negative allows one to experience the energy fields of that which is positive. It is only the removal of the negative that is necessary—the willingness to let go of the habits of negative thinking. The removal of the obstacles to the experiencing of this will result in an increasing sense of aliveness and a joy of one's own existence." ~David R. Hawkins, MD, Ph.D

Okay, so I know what my inner frequency is. Now what?

That's a wonderful question! If you now understand that you're an energetic match to some things that aren't going to help you live that life of prosperity you're after, it's really important to get rid of that energy.

So, how do you do that?

There are so many different ways, or methods called "modalities" of clearing lower energetic vibrations. My favorite modality, and the one that I use on myself, my family and my clients, is one I developed called Energetic Connections. It is the fastest, most comprehensive method I've come across to clear away those energetic "clouds of negativity" so the true you can shine through. It's simple, straightforward, and miraculous in its effects!

True confessions: I am a recovering people pleaser. My favorite joke about that is, "I am a recovering people pleaser. Is that okay?" Growing up and into my adult years I was always afraid of other's judgments of me, and so I tried really hard to keep my nose clean, so to speak. Though I didn't become a doormat for people, I said yes many times when I should have said no, I would "pretzel" myself and my schedule so no one else was put out, and I had a very hard time ever asking for help because I didn't want to inconvenience anyone.

So, you can imagine my delight when I discovered that I can simply, quickly and easily release the fear of other's judgment! The first time I used energy work to clear that belief, I felt this relief wash over me. It was amazing! It was so fast and so simple. Since I've released the energy of that belief, I have much stronger, healthier boundaries, I don't take things personally like I used to, and there is so much less drama in my life!

It's beyond the scope of this book to dive into the mechanics of Energetic Connections, but I do teach it live in a masterclass called The Prosperity Approach Live: 3 Day Intensive. If you're looking for something that you can learn very quickly and feel its positive effects immediately, please visit my website allysonchavez.com. It has changed my life, my family's life, and my clients' lives for the better.

The other method I'll use on occasion is called Emotional Freedom Technique, (EFT), or "tapping" as it's commonly known. Energy moves at the speed of a thought, and we can clear energy long distance and even for other people, because we're all energy and we're all connected energetically. But sometimes our body really wants to be involved when releasing that energy. After all, the energy is being quarantined in the body, isn't it? That's one of the reasons I like tapping so much. It involves the body in a really easy way.

In a nutshell, tapping on specific "meridian points"—pathways that your energy runs along, much like blood vessels and arteries are the pathways for your blood—while addressing a specific negative emotion, will release that emotion very quickly. It's a simple process you can use on yourself anytime and virtually anywhere. And since emotions are simply indicators of where we're vibrating, releasing the emotion of a situation or belief releases the energy of it, and you are left feeling lighter, more hopeful, more peaceful and balanced; plus you're much more aligned with the prosperity you desire!

I go into much deeper detail with this process in my three month online course called Prosperity Essentials. If you'd like more information about Tapping, you can do a YouTube search for "Tapping" and a myriad of videos will pop up for you.

My favorite website for EFT is www.emofree.com. Gary Craig is the founder of EFT, and this is his website. He walks you through the theory, science and different uses for EFT in a very user-friendly way. Nick and Jessica Ortner have also written many books about EFT and hold a Tapping conference online every year. You can visit their website at www.thetappingsolution.com

Something you can do right now on your own to release lower vibrations of energy is to heighten your awareness of what you're feeling, trace it back to the thought that caused it, and ask yourself what the gift is in the situation, if you're willing to let part or all of the negative experience go energetically. You can even muscle test the level of your willingness! If you're willing, take a deep breath and tap on your breastbone five times, and then let out that energy in a big exhale. You can do this as many times as you require to feel relief. Usually two or three nice big breaths will do it for me.

Chapter 4

Mental: The Second Pillar of Prosperity

———————•———————

Law, not confusion, is the dominating principle in the universe . . . This being so, man has but to right himself to find that the universe is right. And during the process of putting himself right, he will find that as he alters his thoughts towards things and other people, things and other people will alter towards him."

—James Allen

A re you a journey or destination kind of person? Do you find joy in the journey, or would you rather skip the journey and get right to the destination? Before I discovered the prosperity formula I was all about skipping the journey and getting right to the destination. I was impatient for my dreams to come true! I wanted them to come yesterday. But when I discovered the universal and mental laws behind prosperity, and I learned what was truly going on around me and within me, I began enjoying the journey. In fact, the journey became a ton of fun and incredibly magical!

It's important to fully understand that prosperity is a process, not an event. It doesn't have to be a very long process, but there are things that must happen first before you can outwardly experience the life you desire. Prosperity also has specific rules regarding how to create it. These rules revolve around universal laws of thought and creation, which we'll go into detail coming up. As you come to know and obey the rules of prosperity you begin to change, and then life begins to change. But the inner change comes first, the outer change always follows the inner change.

If you feel impatient about creating the life you want, that impatience is simply a mask for an underlying belief that what you want will not actually come, or maybe it will come but it won't stay. That's why most people don't like the journey. They're afraid of it! They're afraid it will be hard and scary, and even after all that work they won't actually get what they want. I speak from experience. I remember going to a week-long training, and at the very beginning on day one, wishing we were at day five and that I knew everything they were going to teach us! I wanted it downloaded in my brain without the experience of learning it. That's how much I didn't like the journey.

Most people are control freaks, whether they admit it or not. That's why I love the mental pillar of prosperity so much! Control freaks rejoice! You get to be as controlling as you can handle with this pillar. The problem most of us have is that we're trying to control the *wrong* things. We're trying to control other people and circumstances, when the only thing within our absolute control is our own thoughts and reactions to circumstances around us.

This chapter is all about pulling back the curtain on your circumstances and your mind to see what's *really* going on. It's about taking a peek into the laws God has created to assist us in being co-creators of our life on this planet. These are universal laws of truth, which means if they work for me they'll also work for you. As you come to know and obey these laws with exactness, you will find life become more and more miraculous. Opportunities will come your way, important connections will be made, and things will work out better than you could ever plan! Don't get too caught up on the word "exactness," though. Exactness doesn't mean perfection. It means doing something with accuracy or correctness.

Obedience brings blessings. But obedience with exactness brings miracles.
–David A. Bednar

In my years of study and research I've found four mental laws and twenty-one universal laws that assist us in creating prosperity. These laws help us clearly see what is really going on around us and our role in creating our reality. When used correctly, these laws help us to feel confident, faithful, and patient throughout the prosperity process. And using these laws helps us to feel joy in the journey, the joy God intended us to feel.

These laws are not an exhaustive list, but they're the ones that I found to be most useful for prosperity. I learned these laws from many amazing teachers along the way, and many online searches, along with lots of prayer and pondering over how they worked in my own life.

Guidelines vs. Rules

In the movie, "The Pirates of the Caribbean" Elizabeth saves her own life by invoking parlez after being captured by pirates, which is the right to speak and negotiate with the captain, rather than just being killed outright. Later on the pirates tell her that parlez "is more of a guideline than an actual rule."

Now any time my husband or I see someone break the law by speeding through a red light or not signaling and then cutting someone off, we joke that the laws are "guidelines more than actual rules."

How many times have you broken the law and not been disciplined for it? For me, too many times to count. (I really like to drive fast!) We tend to think that universal laws act just like man-made laws: sometimes they're invoked and other times they're not. But that's not how the universal laws of thought and creation work.

These laws are as absolute as the laws of math and physics. It doesn't matter who you know, how good you are at talking your way out of things, or even how good of a person you are. If you step off a tall building, the law of gravity is going to pull you down to the earth! And it doesn't matter if you're two years old and you don't know the law, or if you're forty-two and you're ignoring the law. The laws work whether you know them or not, whether you use them or not, or whether you like them or not.

If you make a mistake in math, the error is on your side, not on math. You must correct your mistake, because the laws of math aren't going to change for you. Keep this in mind as you learn these laws. If you're not living the life of prosperity you want it's because you're not obeying the universal laws with exactness. The change must be made on your part, the laws work perfectly every time.

Laws to get you going

I've grouped the laws into two categories: the ones to use when you have a new goal or desire you're working toward, and laws to use when it seems like nothing is working. The laws don't have to be used in order, and you'll see how they dovetail into each other so beautifully! As you read, I invite you to determine how well you obey the laws, and see how the laws are playing out in your life today. You'll find that not every law is applicable in every single situation in your life, so it's not necessary to employ every law all the time. That's why I separated them into two categories.

Law of Perpetual Transmutation: Everything is either going into physical form or out of it. The form it takes depends on the condition of the environment.

Take water, for example. Water exists in many forms: vapor, a gas in the form of steam, rain, and as a solid in ice or snow. But conditions have to be right for it to exist in any of those forms. Rain doesn't always turn to snow. In fact, rain clouds don't always bring rain. The conditions in the environment aren't always conducive to rain. Water can go through a few of these forms without going through all of them, and it can shift back and forth between forms. It has to have the right environment for it to exist in a specific form.

Our ideas work the same way. The level of prosperity you want to develop is, in its beginning state, invisible to the physical word. It's just as real in your mind as it will be when you experience it on the physical plane, the only thing different is its *form*. As long as you hold this idea of prosperity in the right environment long enough, it will show up in your physical world. And where is that environment? Right in your mind. And how do you get it to show up? With belief!

As you hold onto your idea and believe you can experience it, you'll start to move toward it through action. By continuing to do this, your prosperity idea is gathering more energy and getting "heavier," if you will. It's getting more substance behind it. Once you have enough energy behind it, it will turn into matter. This will start when the circumstances you need to get this idea into physical form will begin to present themselves. As you imagine what life will look like and feel like once you've reached prosperity, you're gathering more energy to your idea. And expressing gratitude for it *as if it's already here* makes it more and more "real" to you in your mind. As you do this, you're literally attracting prosperity to you! You'll have ideas come into your mind that will lead you to take action. Many times it's a small action to take, so don't be deceived by its size

I had a small thought come to me when business was pretty slow to text a friend about any job openings where we used to work together. I didn't want to admit that I was having challenges with my business, but I swallowed my pride and asked anyway. Naturally, she asked how business was doing. I told her I was looking to speak on more stages and she asked if I thought about writing a book. Well yes, as a matter of fact, I had! Her brother-in-law just "happened" to be a publisher. She connected us, I submitted him the outline for this book, it was a fit for what he wanted, and now you have this book in your hands. All from one "small" thought.

Faith and belief that your idea will manifest is essential to bringing it into physical form. This is what creates the right environment for it to take form.

Just as faith and belief literally bring your prosperity to you, fear, doubt and disbelief will literally repel it from you. Entertaining those things takes energy away from your desire and causes you to lose focus on what you want. They distract, discourage, and destroy the environment that your idea needs to be able to grow, thrive and manifest physically.

I love the old 1980 live action movie "Popeye," starring Robin Williams. There is a character shown at the beginning of the movie who has dropped his hat and as he's moving forward to pick it up, he inadvertently kicks it. He ends up chasing his hat all over town, because he keeps kicking it away when he's so close to reaching it. That's what happens when you give space for fear, doubt or disbelief to take over. You're kicking your prosperity away from you when you're so close to picking it up!

Create the environment that will be healthy for your prosperity to manifest. Be enthusiastic, be believing, act on the small, large, and even scary ideas that come to you that align with your goal. Express gratitude for it as if it's already here. Spend time imagining what life will look and feel like once your goal is yours. Keep doubt, fear and disbelief at bay. Remember, "When I have a choice, I choose to believe."

Law of Vibration: Everything is in a state of vibration, and that vibration is a medium or vehicle for transferring signals.

Remember my favorite Einstein quote, about everything is energy and that's all there is to it? I'll refresh your memory:

"Everything is energy and that's all there is to it. Match the frequency of the reality you want and you cannot help but get that reality. It can be no other way. This is not philosophy. This is physics."

This quote helps me anchor in the law of vibration really quickly. Everything is in a specific state of vibration, *including the prosperity you want.* The only reason you're not experiencing it in your physical reality is that you're not a vibrational match to it. Yet.

Everything that's going on around you physically is a vibrational match to you, whether you consciously like it or not. Since we live in this universe of vibration and attraction, only those signals that are a match to ours will come into our experience.

So, here we are, walking around emitting a frequency at all times, not even aware that we're doing it. Our vibrations "bump up" against other vibrations in the form of people, events, opportunities, and so forth. If it's a match, it will join us in our journey. If it's not, we'll either not even notice it—why do opportunities always come to "lucky" ones, but not to me?—or we'll notice it and quickly dismiss it—that could never work for me, I wouldn't even know what to do!

> *"The outer conditions of a man's life will always be found to be harmoniously related to his inner state...The soul attracts that which it secretly harbors; that which it loves, and also that which it fears. Men do not attract that which they want, but that which they are."—James Allen*

If you want to change the circumstances you're in, you must tune into another "station" with your vibration. You must change *your vibration*. Most people do it backwards: they wait for the circumstance to change before they'll even consider changing. ("If such and such thing happens, *then* I'll be happy.") But that's not how the laws work, and you'll find yourself more and more frustrated as you wait for your dream to come down to your level of vibration, instead of consciously shifting your inner frequency so that it's an energetic match for what you want.

When we bought our first home, we were house poor for a long time. Our multi-level home was perfect for Christmas lights, but we never had the money around Christmas time to get them. And once was Christmas ended, we still didn't have money to buy them on clearance. Part of the "problem" was that we wanted a very specific look on our home: red, green and white lights only. That would require buying extra sets of lights so my husband could change out the orange and blue bulbs with the colors and the pattern we wanted. And I felt we couldn't afford that. (Beware, feelings and words are powerful!)

However, every January I would think to myself, "This year it's going to be different! This year we're going to make more money so we can have Christmas lights on the house!" I said this for a number of years, but Christmas came and went with our little home devoid of cheerful Christmas lights. Our physical circumstances couldn't change from year to year, because *my vibration* didn't change! I had no idea how we could get Christmas lights, so I didn't give any thought to it, other than to say what I wanted. Just declaring what I wanted wasn't enough to change my vibration to a state that would include having Christmas lights on our home.

It wasn't until I consciously changed my vibration and held it there that we got Christmas lights on our house. But when I did we enjoyed exactly the lights we wanted for years!

The great James Allen also said, "Men are anxious to improve their circumstances, but are unwilling to improve themselves; they therefore remain bound."

How do you change your vibration? I'll show you shortly!

Law of Obedience—You experience life according to your obedience, your understanding and your use of universal laws. Your life is shaped according to how you work with the universal laws.

You will either serve the principle or the physical evidence in all you think and do. The physical evidence that surrounds you can be pretty darn compelling, and most people will look at their circumstances and do their darndest to change them, without understanding the cause that created those circumstances in the first place. It's when we understand the principles, like these universal laws, and begin to obey them that life really starts to change!

Living in ultimate prosperity requires that you obey the principles and not the empirical evidence of your circumstances. Most people obey the evidence, and that's what keeps them from living the life they want.

I recently spoke with a woman who lived with a lot of fear and doubt in her life, and wanted to learn how to change all of that. We had a wonderful conversation as I explained what was lacking and how life is different when she applied the prosperity formula. She expressed a lot of gratitude for my insight, but I invited her to work with me, she immediately listed all the evidence as to why she couldn't. And most of that evidence had to do with money. She had so much fear wrapped up in letting go of money that when the opportunity came to her to change all of that, she let the money stop her. (Most people do this.) She wanted to change her money story but felt she couldn't do that until her money story changed. And that's how most of us stay stuck. I was sad for her when we finished the call, because I knew that she was only going to create more of what she already had. Her *circumstance* –or physical evidence--said she didn't have a lot of money, but the *principle*—the truth—is that she is surrounded by abundance and prosperity! Her experience of life will only change once she begins to follow the principle.

Law of Sacrifice—something always has to be sacrificed for something else. Sacrifice is letting go of something of a lower nature so you can receive something of a higher nature.

I used to really struggle with the law of sacrifice. I'd often heard sacrifice described as "giving up something good for something better." But the problem was, many times when I "sacrificed," I didn't end up with something better! I liked the good—what if the better never came?

But we're using the law of sacrifice all day, every single day. Because we live in linear time, doing one thing necessitates giving up something else. You can't eat at Ruth's Chris while simultaneously eating at McDonald's. You can't watch a movie and attend a concert. One must be sacrificed for the other.

If you want to be physically healthy and fit, you must sacrifice some sleeping time to move your body. You'll have to change your eating habits and drink lots of water. At first, is that sacrifice hard? Sure! It can definitely feel challenging, especially if your body loves what you're currently doing! But over time, when you have more energy, when your skin glows, you sleep better, and you get to buy smaller sizes, does it feel so much like a sacrifice? Not at all! You traded the lower for the higher. Sacrifice is just "trading up."

My client Karen was a wonderful example of using the law of sacrifice. Karen came to me because she was tired of living on the edge of panic every day. She was sleeping walking at night, was snappish with her kids, impatient with her husband, and feeling stagnant in her own growth. Money was a constant worry, and Karen was ready to change that.

As we worked together, she began investing more in herself and her personal development. She began teaching her children new ways to think. Her level of panic significantly decreased so that she was sleeping better. She adopted better eating habits, then trained for and ran half marathons! And because of all of Karen's sacrifice, her family was able to move out of their unsafe neighborhood into a home and neighborhood that was much nicer. Karen did a lot of "sacrificing". She said, "I carried around a lot of money issues, anxiety issues and self-worth issues…This has made a huge difference! I'm feeling better and sleeping better! Allyson brought this into my life at the perfect time!"

It was inspiring to watch how much Karen grew as we worked together. She acted in spite of her fear and wonderful results came from that. She was willing to trade up!

When growth opportunities come that initially may make you feel frightened or unsure about your ability to be successful, ask if where you currently are will get you what you want. If not, be willing to trade up.

"If you want to move to a higher level of life, you have to be willing to let go of some of your old ways of thinking and being and adopt new ones. The results will eventually speak for themselves."

–T. Harv Eker

Law of Cause & Effect (aka the Law of the Harvest)

For every cause there is a definite effect, and for every effect there is a definite cause. Your thoughts, behaviors and actions create specific effects that manifest and create your life as you know it. Effects don't happen randomly.

To drive this law home a little bit easier, I substituted the word "results" for "effects." So, the law can read: "for every cause there is a definite result, and for every result there is a definite cause. Results don't happen randomly."

This law has a perfect illustration: if you plant carrot seeds you will never, ever, ever get a tulip. You'll always get a carrot. Now, the size of the carrot, its vibrancy or nutritional value all depend on the quality of the soil in which you plant it, but you can be absolutely certain that planting a carrot seed will result in a carrot.

How does this law play out in our everyday lives? Let's use a work project as an example. If you plant seeds of doubt, then every time you work on your project you're going to be second guessing the decisions you're making, you'll have a hard time making decisions, you'll wonder if what you're doing is enough and hope to high heaven that everything will turn out all right. When show time comes you'll either overcompensate for feeling insecure by putting on a big bravado, or you'll shrink back and hide a bit. The results of that project will either be less than what you had hoped for, or if the project is really successful, you'll wonder if it's a fluke!

I have personal experience planting seeds of doubt alongside my dreams. I think all of us do. I remember when I first started my coaching business how much self-doubt filled me. I didn't really expect to sign clients, and every time I did, I wondered if it was a fluke. And this wasn't just after the first or second client I signed—I thought it was a fluke every single time! My results were never as high as I was aiming for, so there was always a bit of disappointment mingled in with the celebration. My results came directly from the cause, and the cause was my doubt around my ability to be successful signing clients.

On the other hand, my brother Tim plants seeds of *certainty*. He has a successful business and is constantly thinking of ways to make it even more successful. He proudly showed me an all-terrain utility vehicle he had at his house at one time. He paid $10,000 for it and said he was using it in a contest/raffle for his customers. He had no idea if the investment would pay off, but he acted as if it would. He and his team worked diligently for 6 weeks, and by the end of the contest period he had created an additional $400,000 in sales. Now *that* is a seed worth planting!

Dennis R. Deaton, author of *The Book on Mind Management*, has said, "Most of what shows up in the world around you is an effect which has been caused by your thoughts. You are the cause. You are such a powerful cause, most of the effects you experience are of your personal production."

I know most people balk at that. "What? *I caused* all the drama going on around me? *I caused* my teenager to be mouthy? *I caused* this financial turmoil? That can't be right! I'm working so hard, trying so hard." Yet, it's true. Are there other players in your life's game? Of course. But they wouldn't be behaving the way they are or stirring up the drama if *you weren't an energetic match* in the first place. The faster you come to accept that, the faster you'll claim how powerful you are, and the faster your life can change!

Law of Attention (aka Law of Focus)

Whatever you focus and give your attention to will manifest. What you focus on expands.

Energy flows where attention goes. Attention is the focus of your thoughts, words and actions. If you want to stop flowing energy to things you don't want, shift your attention to things you do want. If all you're focused on is the disaster you're trying to avoid, where are you headed? Right toward the disaster!

For several years I was in charge of the girls aged twelve through eighteen in my church's congregation. Every year we'd go to girls' camp. I remember one year we drove down to southern Utah for camp.

One of the day activities was spent at the lake boating, playing in the water, and paddleboarding. I'd never ridden a paddleboard before, and I was excited to try it out! I noticed a tree out in the water, which I really didn't want to get tangled in. But as I looked at the tree, I continued to paddle right towards it. I hadn't mastered the art of steering the paddleboard yet, and so what happened? Yep! I went right into that tree. The girls got quite a kick out of watching me go straight into that tree, but I managed to keep a hold of the paddle, stay up right on the board, and finally get out of the branches.

When you have your goal in front of you but see obstacles, do whatever you must to stay focused on the goal. Give as little attention to the obstacles as possible. If you focus on the obstacle, that's all you'll get. Pay attention to where your thoughts generally lead you.

I had a client once who leaned toward being dramatic. If things weren't going perfectly, her life was a catastrophe. As she learned about the Law of Attention, I encouraged her to use it to her advantage and only focus on what she wanted. She agreed, and a very short time later had the opportunity to put this law into practice. (The universe is very accommodating with that, I've found!)

Later on, she told me about the experience. She'd had a disgruntled client send her an email that was rude, nasty and unjustified. Normally she would have fired off her own reactive email, then called her husband, texted her girlfriends and put a lot of attention on this negativity. But this time she remembered the Law of Attention. She didn't want to put any more energy into the situation than was already there, so she resisted texting or calling anyone, and even shut down her computer and walked away instead of answering the email. She did admit it was really hard to do, because all she wanted was to defend her own innocence. But she stayed committed and didn't tell anyone about the experience. Later that day she answered the email politely and professionally, and the situation resolved itself easily and naturally. And she felt poised and calm as she focused on what she *did* want instead of pumping energy into what she didn't want.

Time to get into some awareness!

Write down the main thing you've given your attention to today.

_____

_____

Is that attention leading you one small step closer to your dream or one small step away from it? (Write it below. Be honest and objective. This is for awareness purposes only.)

_____

_____

Law of Non-Resistance: What you resist, persists. Don't fight the obstacles or resist the situation you're in. When you resist it, you'll always have it with you.

Don't work against things you don't want; instead, work toward those things you do want. This means don't give your time, energy, and attention to people or things that oppose what you want. You're creating barriers to your prosperity coming in. Instead, be like the little stream. Let me explain.

Water is so powerful, and yet it's the perfect non-resistant element. It can take the shape of any container it's in. It wears away the hardest rock. Nothing can withstand the force of a tsunami. But how does a big river begin? As a little stream high in the mountains. And it starts as a crooked little stream, running into boulders and branches as it makes its way down the mountain. What does the water do when it comes up against those obstacles? It just winds its way around them! It doesn't call in the troops or try to build up enough force to push the boulder or the tree out of the way; it simply goes around! And yes, it winds back and forth, and sometimes doubles back on itself, but is it still getting toward its goal? Of course!

When most people come up against a boulder in their own lives, they immediately stop their progress, collect their forces and put up a fight to get it out of the way. (This sounds a lot like, "I've got to figure this out.") This resistance they've set up causes friction. And friction causes irritation and inflammation. Friction is opposition and resistance.

When I first saw my business going downhill, you can bet I resisted that! I did everything I could think of to try to drum up more clients and more sales. I hired mentors, took more trainings, all in a desperate attempt to keep the business afloat. It wasn't wrong of me to hire mentors or increase my training; that's part of what brings high levels of success. But the energy I was in was a fighting energy. My prayers were filled with pleading to take this away and save me. I didn't see until after I stopped resisting that everything was happening to help me get back on my purpose so I could teach what I was sent here to teach. The Prosperity Approach didn't come to me until *after* I quit fighting and resisting. The castle I had built needed to be dismantled to make room for the empire that would come in its place.

Going through life arguing, fighting, resenting and judging puts more obstacles in your path. You get so preoccupied fighting those obstacles that you lose sight of your real objective. So, don't make a big deal out of the obstacle; keep your eye on the prize, and persevere. You might have to wind around and around those obstacles, but you will ultimately win. Let go of the temptation to worry, complain, doubt yourself, be swallowed by fear or get angry and frustrated. Those are boulders that will stop you every time.

What you resist, persists.

List some things that cause friction or resistance for your goal. Example: worrying, arguing, judging

1.

2.

3.

4.

5.

Law of Flow: Everything is always moving and changing, flowing in and out of life. To allow new things to come in, you must let go of the old.

Here is a physics lesson, explained so a five-year-old can understand: when something is full, there is no room for anything else to come in! If you want new experiences with prosperity, you must let go of old stories, emotions, resentments, and even physical items to allow the new to come in. When you hang onto money, clothes, jewelry and even old emotions, there is no room for anything new to come in. Holding onto old memories and emotions that don't serve you blocks new, refreshing things from flowing in. As soon as you throw those things away, the law of flow ensures something else will come in to take its place.

It's important to note that you get to choose whether to replace those emotions with the same emotions, or shift your thinking to attract something better. If you have the same thoughts and beliefs, you'll stay in the same inner frequency or vibration, and the same conditions will return.

For thirty years I held onto massive amounts of grief at losing my mom. Though I didn't cry every day, anytime one of my aunts would talk about her, or my brothers would mention her, my throat would close up and my eyes would fill with tears. I was continually surprised at this—why was I still so emotional about something that happened so far in the past? Though we hadn't been allowed to mourn losing her, in my adult life I'd done immense amounts of healing around losing a loved one. Though I knew part of me would always grieve, I thought I'd moved most of it out.

It wasn't until I was working with another energy practitioner that I realized what was going on. I was releasing grief, but then I would immediately call it back with my thoughts and emotions. My body was *filled* with grief! It wasn't until after I chose to let that grief go and replace it with feelings of hope and peace, that those new emotions could actually stay with me.

This is how I knew most of the grief had been released: I could cry in a very deep way and it didn't feel like my heart was breaking again. Any time I'd cried in my life, no matter what I was crying about, it felt like my heart was seizing. But now I can cry and feel deep emotions, and my heart feels strong and whole. I had no idea what that felt like until then.

The example I gave above is extreme. The changes don't have to be big like the one I described. Even if the change is small, it's enough. Something different has to come in. Don't be really concerned with the *size* of the change, but the *quality* of the change.

Another exercise!

Think about one situation, emotional or physical, that is not flowing well. What is one thing you can do to activate the Law of Flow? Write it below.

_____

_____

_____

Vacuum Law of Prosperity: Nature abhors a vacuum. When empty space is created, nature always moves in to fill it.

The Law of Prosperity is what I call the "physical counterpart" to the Law of Flow. This is a law you can utilize immediately and see how it works. Do you have a closet or a junk drawer? Clean it out! You'll feel the shift immediately, both inside you and inside your physical environment. Don't you take a big sigh of relief and look around in satisfaction when the house is all clean? Doesn't it *feel* so good?

When my mind feels cluttered, I look around my physical environment. Invariably, it's cluttered as well. Marianne Williamson said, "A cluttered desk is the sign of a distressed mind." Once I clean up my desk and my office the ideas start flowing again. This also works for money.

I love the story Bob Proctor tells about a time when he visited his aunt. She complained about the ugly drapes that hung in her living room, exclaiming how embarrassed she was but she couldn't afford new ones. Bob finally told her, "Auntie, you love those drapes! New drapes can't come in until you get rid of those. There is no space for them."

She decided to test his theory. The next time he saw her, new drapes hung proudly in her living room, and her living room was empty of furniture!

His aunt used the Law of Prosperity to discard her old drapes so there would be physical room for new ones. When she saw that the first experiment worked, she got rid of her living room furniture to make room for new furniture to take its place.

Using the Law of Prosperity by physically getting rid of things that you no longer use by donating them or throwing them away, shows *active faith.* You don't know how or when that space will be filled, but I guarantee you it will be filled. Why do you think people spring clean their closets *every year?*

One of my clients, Courtney, used the Law of Prosperity when she and her husband wanted to adopt a baby. After they became certified to adopt, they began to physically prepare for a baby. They cleaned out the spare bedroom and painted it the color they wanted for the nursery, set up the furniture and got everything ready, knowing full well that the adoption process could take years. Regardless of that, they made room, without desperation or pleading or demanding the time frame, sex of the child, or even if one would come. But they spoke about having a child, made physical room for a baby in their family, and *within five months* they adopted!

Question for you:

Where can you physically create space in your life for something better to come in and fill it?

_____

_____

Laws to Use When it Seems Like Nothing is Working

All right! You've got your goal or vision in front of you, you're thinking about how great it will be once that dream has arrived, you're keeping frustration and impatience at bay, you've cleaned out your closets, you're keeping your thoughts on the prize and moving around obstacles. But your goal isn't here yet. Now what do you do? Keep these other laws in mind and do what they tell you to do!

Law of Gestation: Every seed has an incubation period. It takes time for an idea to develop and reach maturity. We don't always know how long it will be, but it is finite. It comes to an end. Our ideas never come faster than the period of time it takes for them to mature.

If you're keeping your thoughts in check, and you're feeling better but nothing outside of you has really changed, keep doing what you're doing! We live in time lag on this planet. We have to create in linear time here. If your prosperity is not here yet, it could be simply that you're in gestation. The baby is coming!

I have four children. My first child was born eight days *late*. And when I delivered a 9 lb 6 oz baby boy, you can bet I wished the gestation period had ended two weeks before it did. But he was healthy and fully developed. He was perfect! My third child came seven weeks *early*. He weighed in at 3 lbs 14 oz. And thankfully, he was healthy. But his lungs weren't fully developed and I had to have a steroid shot before he was born to speed up that development. His sucking reflex hadn't developed yet, so he had a feeding tube the first three weeks of his life until he grew enough for that reflex to kick in. We could only hold him for an hour a day because he couldn't hold his body temperature. He needed that extra time to mature inside before he was fully prepared to make a physical entrance in the outside world. But because he didn't get that extra time, complications arose.

The Law of Gestation is vital. You don't want to rush it along, because you might get a half-baked dream with a lot of complications. This is the time to prepare yourself to be able to receive the prosperity you're after. If it's not here yet, it's because either you or it is not ready for physical form yet. Stay patient. Keep going!

There really is no such thing as an overnight success. Gestation plays a role in every person's dreams. Steve Jobs said, "If you look really closely, most overnight successes took a long time."

Law of Sufficiency and Abundance: You have everything inside you right now to create the life you desire. You are literally surrounded by abundance that is yours for the taking.

When you can look at what currently *is* in your reality, and feel satisfaction and gratitude for what you currently have while still looking forward to greater things, you'll end up manifesting those more quickly.

But what if you're not experiencing all you expected to by now? What if things haven't turned around yet and still feel really hard? How can you be satisfied with that? There are a number of things you can do that are simple and fast and have a lasting effect. Playing a game I call *"What's working for me now?"* was instrumental in pulling me from despair after my business collapsed. This game also happens to immediately activate the Law of Sufficiency and Abundance.

Early one winter morning I was on my way to assist in an event, trying so hard to keep it together. All I wanted to do was crawl back in bed and sob all day long. Since I was going to be on stage in front of a room full of people, it was vital that I have high energy and enthusiasm. And it just wasn't there. Telling myself *not to cry* only made my eyes fill with tears, so I knew I had to act fast before I was a complete mess. I asked myself the question, "What is working for me right now in this moment?" The heater was on in my van, so I was warm on a bitterly cold day. That was working for me. My hair looked good, so that was working for me. I had comfortable shoes on. The stereo worked. I'd eaten breakfast, so my stomach was content. That was working for me. The van was a reliable vehicle, so that was working for me. The day was cold and bitter, but the sky was clear and the sun was shining. It was beautiful! There was no traffic. And most importantly, the heated leather seat I was sitting on was working, and my butt was warm. (Can't you face anything if your butt is warm?)

I glanced at the clock when I started this exercise, and then looked again when I started to feel better. It took *two minutes* to pull myself from a state of falling apart to smiling, comfortable, and looking forward to the day ahead and playing full out.

During this exercise, I only focused on what was in my *immediate environment* that was working for me. I didn't think about my problem or my despair at all. I focused on the complete opposite, but something that I could physically connect to in that moment. And those things I connected to were simple and mostly inconsequential. But in that moment they all served to connect me with the fact that *I had everything I needed in that moment to succeed.* In that moment I was taken care of in every way. Every need was met. And some exceeded my expectations (note my warm backside)!

By definition, sufficiency is "an adequate amount of something, especially of something essential." (dictionary.com)

Once I connected to the sufficiency around me that was supporting me in that very moment, I calmed down and began looking forward to better things coming. And I had a remarkable day!

Understand also that you live in a world and a universe that is abundant and constantly expanding. You are literally surrounded by abundance! The more you can connect with that abundance and *feel it,* the faster you'll change your circumstances.

Nature is the perfect example. We see abundance everywhere. Try counting the leaves on just one branch of a tree, or the blades of grass in a square foot. Have you ever picked up a handful of sand and tried to count it? You lose count pretty soon because there is so much of it! There is evidence God has placed all around us that we live in abundance. He takes care of the earth abundantly. You are His crowning achievement, His greatest creation. He will take care of you abundantly to the degree that you will connect to Him and *receive* the goodness He has for you.

When you're satisfied with your conditions and can find peace and gratitude in your life no matter what your circumstances are, you're in the perfect position to manifest what you really want to experience.

List some ways you feel satisfied and grateful for life right now:

_____

_____

_____

_____

Now get brave and list what you'd really like to experience right now:

_____

_____

The Law of Detachment: In order to successfully attract something, you must be detached from the outcome.

This law feels counterintuitive at first blush. "What? You mean in order to be successful attracting something I have to be okay if it doesn't come?" And yes, that's exactly how this law works.

If your sense of worth or your happiness depends on having something, you are sending out the vibration of *attachment*. Attachment is based in fear and scarcity and sends out negative emotions of fear, doubt, or craving (also described as *need*), which literally repels what it is you want. If the Law of Sufficiency and Abundance is correct, that you *already* have within you *everything* you need to create the prosperity of your dreams, then there is nothing to worry about, and there is nothing to be attached to. When you're attached to something or someone, it has the ability to manipulate or control you. Essentially, you're placing your power outside of you and connecting to something other than your Higher Power. One of my mentors used to call it a "power leak."

When something has to *look* a certain way for you to receive it, it shuts out a whole range of possibilities. When you look to outside sources to bring you fulfillment, you are giving your power away. When you detach from the outcome, it ceases to have power over you, and you have complete power over it.

Do you have power over your bank account, or does it own you? Regardless of the amount in your account, if your predominant emotions are negative and fearful, you're attached to it. And it will become very hard to sustain or grow more in that account because of those dominant emotions. You attract whatever your dominant emotions are. Remember the Law of Cause and Effect? If it's worry, fear and doubt you're sending out, you'll get a vibrational match in return.

How do you know if you're attached to something? If you feel like you're trying to "push the river" or *make* it happen, you're attached. Anytime you're worried or anxious is a sure sign you're attached to a specific outcome. When you think to yourself, "I want this SO BAD!" you're attached. Instead, try thinking, "I'm so excited to see how this comes!" Does that feel better to you?

On the flip side, what does being unattached look like in your everyday life? It looks like setting your intention and taking inspired action (which comes in the form of ideas and opportunities that lead you one step closer to your goal), but letting go of *when and how* it's going to be delivered to you. *Those* are the things you detach from. Activate the Law of Perpetual Transmutation in your life by focusing on faith, belief and joyful expectation that it's coming, while keeping impatience, doubt and frustration at bay. This allows much more to flow your way, and for God to bring you miracles in very clever and creative ways. "Assume the sale," which in this case means operate from the space that the prosperity you're working toward *will* manifest, and keep going until it does!

Before I started my online business, I worked in the direct sales industry for thirteen years. Ideally, I would have loved to end that career and immediately be successful in my brand new business. That's not how it played out. There was a six month transition period I needed to be able to pay our bills and start up my new company. I continued to work in direct sales and my new business, and though I preferred the money to come from my new business, for quite a while I'd get unexpected deposits that came from orders placed on my old website.

We always had enough to pay our bills, and that was end goal. If I had been really attached to *where* that money came from, it would have shut down an income channel for me. So, even though I preferred that it come from my new business, I let go of that and was just grateful it came at all! The end goal was met (we had money to pay our bills) and I let go of *how* it came and *when* it came.

Law of Attraction: What you send out vibrationally, you will receive back in the form of people, events, circumstances and situations that are a vibrational match to you. Similar energies are drawn together. Like attracts like.

The Law of Attraction is the most well-known universal law, and there are so many people who teach how to create only using the Law of Attraction. Focusing exclusively on this law paints an incomplete picture, however. This is mostly a default law, like the law of gravity. You attract what you send out. Your friends are your friends because you're a vibrational match. Have you noticed that the people you hang out with make roughly the same amount of money as you, have similar circumstances as you, and think the way you do? It's not so much that you have a ton in common; it's really that you're all on the same vibrational frequency.

James Allen, who wrote *As a Man Thinketh* in the early 20th century, said, "The outer conditions of a person's life will always be found to be harmoniously related to his inner state. The soul attracts that which it secretly harbors; that which it loves, and also that which it fears…Men do not attract that which they want, but that which they are."

How do you use this law when nothing's working in your life? By getting into awareness of what it is you're sending out in terms of dominant thoughts and feelings. Awareness is the first step to changing anything. So just notice what you think about the most and how you normally feel. And if you don't like what you're thinking or how you're feeling, then you get to change both!

One of the reasons 2011 was so difficult for me was that I was misusing the Law of Attraction and didn't even realize it. Before my brother passed away we had been trying to sell our house. For five long months it sat on the market without so much as a whisper of movement. We finally got an interested buyer and even had it under contract, pending appraisal. The appraisal came in and devalued our land so dramatically that it killed the sale. I was devastated and felt powerless against this "nameless man" who, with a flick of his hand, sealed our fate. My thoughts were filled with frustration, victimhood, resentment and anger. Then my brother died in such an unexpected way, which made me feel even *more* powerless. Add in the car engine that died and I was about done for. Is it any surprise that only three days later *the oven caught on fire?* Not to me it isn't! All the seeming catastrophes perfectly matched my inner state. I'm not saying that I magically made the oven burst into flames, but I *was* an energetic match to having more things falling apart.

One of the reasons my business diminished the way it did was due to the signal I was sending out without consciously being aware of it. As I felt more and more worried about losing money, I attracted clients who wouldn't pay for my services. It started off fine, and they made their monthly payments in full and on time. But as I got wobbly, so did their payments. I ended up having to remove half of my clients from my group mentoring program because they weren't paying. That was one of the reasons my business dismantled; clients who didn't pay me and didn't honor the legal contracts they'd signed. But my soul harbored secret fear that I wouldn't be able to sustain high levels of lasting success, and I aligned with the people who supported that particular energetic frequency. The law worked perfectly.

Law of Deliberate Creation: What you think about, you get. So *deliberately choose* to think high vibrating thoughts around what you want to create.

How is Deliberate Creation different from the Law of Attraction? The Law of Attraction creates by default. Your state of emotion and thoughts at any given moment, whether you're aware of it or not, is what you're receiving more of. Deliberate Creation creates by *intention*. With Deliberate Creation you know exactly what vibration you're creating. The Law of Attraction is like a boomerang; the Law of Deliberate Creation is like a bulls-eye.

There are two phases to Deliberate Creation: *desire* and *expectation*.

When you desire something, you literally set up an energetic line of force that connects you with the invisible side of what you want. If your desire weakens or you change it, that particular line of force is disconnected or it misses its goal. But if you stay constant in your desire, you'll sooner or later manifest it, either partially or in whole.

It's no good desiring something unless you expect to get it, either partially or in full. Desire without expectation is nothing more than wishing and is a huge waste of mental energy. Desire puts you in touch and connects you with the frequency of the thing you want. Continuous expectation is what is required to pull it into your physical reality.

Expectation is a very powerful attractive force. It's important to use expectation to your advantage. Never expect a thing you don't want. That is, never tell yourself to hope for the best but expect the worst, because you'll get what you expect more often than not. When you expect something you don't want, you end up attracting what it is you don't want. For example, Zig Ziglar tells the story of a woman who lived in his neighborhood who always complained that she just knew she'd "get the cancer." Every time she said this she always touched one of her breasts. What did she die of? Breast cancer. On the flip side, never *want* a thing you don't *expect* to receive. When you want things you don't expect to receive, you waste valuable mental force. It becomes nothing more than wishful thinking accompanied by a sigh. What a huge waste of mental energy! But when you *constantly expect* the thing that you *persistently desire*, your ability to attract it becomes irresistible.

How do you do this? Live it in your mind! Pretending it's already here is a very simple yet powerful exercise to manifest prosperity that much faster. I was in a mindset class once and one of the students wrote 'pretending' out like this: pre-tending. You are tending that idea in your mind, taking care of that idea—therefore, you are pre-tending it because it hasn't shown up physically yet. It had a profound impact on me! Suddenly pretending everything had all worked out wasn't just an escape or a form of denial: it was a powerful visualization to increase my inner frequency, change my thoughts and emotions and get me energetically aligned with the life I desired.

You use deliberate creation every time you visualize what you want. Dr. Joe Vitale gave a wonderful exercise in his book *The Attractor Factor* that puts you in a state of deliberate creation. He calls it Intentional Meditation. I call it Deliberate Creation at Work! He suggests that every day for thirty days you spend twenty minutes intentionally thinking about how you would like life to be thirty days from now. To do that, simply write out a clear statement that describes what it is you have (for example: at the end of these thirty days, I have twenty new clients, or I've released eight pounds, etc.). It's important that whatever you choose is a bit of a stretch but is also *believable to you*. If you don't believe you can do it, you probably won't. Don't go visualizing winning the lottery or losing fifty pounds in the next month. And then talk to yourself (quietly out loud, or in your mind is fine) about *how it feels to have met that goal*. What does life look like? How do you feel about it? Are you whistling? Are you smiling? How are you celebrating? What are you wearing? How are you showing up? Relish the idea of how it would feel to have it now.

If you can spend twenty minutes a day for thirty consecutive days practicing the art of deliberate creation as described above, you will dramatically increase your powers of manifestation. Why? Because for twenty full minutes you are an energetic match to the reality you wish to experience! In that moment, you are literally changing your future.

Law of Rhythm: Nature's movements are cyclical. There is repetition in everything.

God loves to use nature as the perfect example of how to relate to Him, how He relates to us and will always take care of us, and how true creation actually works. There is a rhythm and an order to everything:

the tide coming in and out, how the planets orbit, the four seasons, even how the sun rises and sets every day. There are different timelines for these things, for example the rhythm of one day is twenty-four hours but the time it takes for the planet to orbit the sun is 365 ¼ days. However, everything has a rhythm.

Our lives are a perfect parallel to this. We have good days and we have bad days. There are times when we prosper, and times when we don't. We experience joy and sadness over and over again throughout our lives.

How does this law help when it seems like nothing is working and everything is falling apart? Realize that by law your circumstances can't continue to go down forever. It has to bottom out and start going up at some point. Even better is knowing that you can actually influence the upturn to come sooner rather than later. If you feel like you're on a down that has no bottom, declare in your mind that you have reached your bottom, and continually grab that better-feeling thought and that better-feeling vibration.

I loved that concept! Imagine my frustration when, after I'd declared that I'd hit rock bottom, circumstances kept going down. I spoke to my mentor about this and she reminded me that circumstances work in time lag, so they have to play out in real time, even after we've declared a new vibration in our thoughts and bodies. So, keep reminding yourself that you've already hit rock bottom in your life and *no matter what circumstances look like*, keep your thoughts UP. Keep connecting and reconnecting to God, trusting that He knows exactly what part of the ride you're on, and that everything will work out.

Comfort yourself with the knowledge and assurance that your down eventually *has* to level out and then swing up, and that eventually this experience will only be a memory.

One of my clients was having a really difficult time in every area of her life, and wanted to give up on her dreams. The problem she was having was connecting to God; she wanted nothing to do with that.

And I have firsthand experience of feeling abandoned by God, so I knew better than to tell her to connect with God anyway! Instead, we focused on different acts of self-love she could do daily, as well as reaching out and serving others during this very low time in her life. I reminded her of what one of my mentors once told me, "When you're in drama, you're in your story. Serving others gets you out of your story." That self-care was vital for her, but so was serving.

Our mentoring together ended while she was still in the "down," and I wasn't there to see the upturn happen. However, I recently received an email from her that said she'd come back to her soul's purpose, felt recommitted to living her passion, and she was healing her relationship with her Higher Power. Things had definitely turned up for her!

What can you do right now to begin an upswing in your thoughts and emotions? Write it below. Examples: listening to music that is inspiring and comforting, declaring that you've reached the bottom and it's only up from here and honoring that declaration in your thoughts

_____

_____

_____

Law of Relativity: Nothing you experience is fundamentally good or bad. Bad things are bad only relative to something better.

I love going to personal development classes as often as possible! In one of the classes I took, I learned that "Nothing has meaning until I give it meaning." This is another way to sum up the Law of Relativity. Most of the meaning we give to our circumstances isn't supportive to our growth and reaching for something better. Most of the time we look at our circumstances and compare them to someone else's better circumstances. That leads to feeling less than satisfied with what we've got, along with feeling frustrated, impatient, and many times, abandoned.

It's in our human nature to compare ourselves to others, or even to ourselves and "how we used to be." If we've put on some weight we definitely tend to compare ourselves with how we used to be. Make sure to use this law to your advantage and *only compare your situation with a worse one*. This will help you be able to hold more faithful thoughts. Find gratitude and the blessings that are in your current circumstances (they're there, by law) to help you feel better about your situation. The idea is to feel grateful about what you have *now*, not feel worse. Remember, we create our future with our dominant thoughts and emotions.

When my brother died so unexpectedly, I remember thinking even in the midst of my grief that it could have been so much worse. If I had to lose a family member, losing an adult brother who had lived a great life and I'd had a wonderful relationship with made it much easier to cope. That was on blessing I *could* see.

Sometimes people take issue with "comparing down", because of their own judgmental voice. It sounds an awful lot like, "You should be grateful to have this experience…at least it's not as bad as…" And many times that just makes us feel worse. Be sure when using this law, that you use it to your advantage. Comparing *down* is meant to help you grasp gratitude for what currently *is*, not shame you because you want something better and "should" be happy for the lot you have. It's meant to assist you in finding hidden blessings more easily.

In his book, *Dad is Fat,* Jim Gaffigan tells a joke about parenting that goes like this, "Raising kids may be a thankless job with ridiculous hours, but at least the pay sucks."

This is *not* using the law of relativity to your advantage! But it's hysterical! And if you're honest with yourself, isn't that what we kind of do when we're in a rough spot? We either play the martyr role (which sounds like "welcome to my life.") or we think about all the things that could be better in our lives, which just make us feel worse about our situation. Instead, think of the ways it could be worse so that you can feel better.

Socrates said, "If all our misfortunes were laid in one common heap whence everyone must take an equal portion, most people would be content to take their own and depart."

This law in action: List five ways your current situation could be worse, and then five blessings that you've received from this situation already!

Compare down

1.

2.

3.

4.

5.

Current blessings in my situation right now

1.

2.

3.

4.

5.

Law of Polarity: Every situation has an opposite that is of equal degree. If your circumstance is kind of bad, it's also kind of good. If your circumstance is absolutely terrible, it is also absolutely incredible at the same time and to the same degree!

Remember, nothing has meaning until you give it meaning. The situation itself isn't good or bad—it just is. If you've put a "bad" label on a situation, start looking for the "good" labels that have to be there, by law. Napoleon Hill said, "Every adversity, every failure and every heartache, carries within it the seed of an equivalent or greater benefit." And while the seeds are certainly there, every adversity, failure and heartache also carries within it advantage, success and delight. It's your job to find them, because they're hidden.

I love the story of two little girls who were put into separate rooms filled with horse manure. The first little girl looked at all that horse manure and promptly began to cry. The second little girl looked at all that manure, whooped for joy and *began digging in it!* When asked what she was doing, she replied, "With all this manure, there's *got* to be a pony in here somewhere!"

Are you sitting in your own poopy situation and crying about it, or are you digging around for the pony that is bound to be there? Use the Law of Polarity to your advantage by looking for your symbolic pony, and you'll actually shorten the time that you're in that tough situation.

As painful as losing that income was, the law of polarity guaranteed that something else just as powerful lurked in that situation, only it was the opposite of painful. And what did I find? The Prosperity Formula! The missing piece to success! I discovered that you need to change your inner stance in all areas of your life--spiritually, energetically, mentally and physically--in order to have a solid foundation under you so you can build something truly lasting. The law of polarity gave me something powerfully positive to focus on other than the financial disaster we were dealing with. And that gave me great comfort and hope for an even brighter future.

Law of Utilization: When you make full use of everything in your life, the bad as well as the good, it leads to manifestation.

I love this law! Utilization leads to manifestation. Another way to describe this law is through this mantra: Everything happens for a reason, and that reason is to assist me. How can I utilize this?

This is so helpful when it seems like life is falling apart, no matter what you're doing to salvage it. When we stop resisting the "bad" that's happening, and allow it to be exactly what it is—a tool to be used for our good and our growth—we begin to see life through different eyes.

Einstein said, "There are two ways to look at life. One is as if nothing is a miracle. The other is as if everything is a miracle." What's the miracle of not being able to pay bills? What's the miracle of not having great health? That's for you to find in your own circumstances.

But I know that as you look around in your life and treat every circumstance as a miracle that is there to assist you, your focus will change. You'll begin to see how much God does love and care for you, as He sends you angels disguised as humans that you can see, and angels that you can't. Some of the sweetest, most cherished experiences of my life have come during the darkest times of my life.

One of my friends was going through a particularly rough time, and she confided in me how better off her kids would be without her. We didn't meet until we were adults, so she didn't know my background. I told her about my childhood and the aftermath of losing a mom who considered her kids better off without her, I could tell her with authority that her children were *not* better off without her, regardless of her mental state. I took an experience that for years had me wondering what good it really did me, and in that moment, I utilized it to save three young girls from going through what I had to go through as a child, and as an adult. My friend told me later that I saved her life that night. If my experience can save just one mama, and just one child, it was worth it.

What if what you have been handed was *exactly what you needed* and was exactly what was *required* to lead you to your dreams? Would that change your perspective? Would you resent it, push against it and feel frustrated by it, or would you use that as a tool to create the life you want? I believe that no matter what you're going through, it's exactly what you need for your growth, and is exactly what is required to create your dreams. It's up to you to use whatever you're handed to your advantage.

Miracle Exercise: What's going on in your life right now that you can utilize for your good? How is a tough time assisting you? Write it below.

_____

_____

_____

Law of Projection: All aspects of ourselves are reflected back to us. All that we perceive outside ourselves is a mirror of something within. Therefore, everything that we see outside is a projection. Otherwise known as: You spot it, you got it.

I'll be honest, this was a tough law for me to wrap my mind around when I first learned about it. Certainly, that woman who drove me crazy because she wouldn't quit talking about herself wasn't a quality *in me* I was recognizing, was it? According to this universal law, that's exactly what it is.

What you see in other people is nothing more than a mirror of your own inner thoughts, feelings and beliefs. And when what you notice elicits an emotional response from you, you can be confident that's the Law of Projection playing out in your life.

So, what do we do when we're triggered negatively by someone? First, celebrate that you've been triggered! This is part of you that is wanting to be acknowledged, loved and embraced. So, humble yourself enough to recognize that what you're seeing and not liking about someone else is the exact same quality you have that you just don't want to see.

To refer back to the example above: I was at a three day event where we were to choose buddies that we'd hang around with the entire three days to do some deep work together. She never asked about me or my situation, all she did was talk about herself. By the end of those three days I was almost crazy! But why was I so upset that she was talking all the time? *Because there was no time to talk about me!* So, at least a part of me wants to do nothing more except talk about myself all the time. And can I accept that as true? Of course! When I saw that I was just like her, and that experience was meant to show how self-centered I can be, it was a powerful lesson. Now, does that give me permission to do nothing but talk about myself all the time? Of course not. But it does give me permission to acknowledge that inner fifteen-year-old whose entire universe revolves around her, and love her and tell her to be patient for her time to talk. At that point I was no longer triggered.

When you learn to heal and embrace those parts of you that you don't like, and develop those gifts that are currently dormant, emotional reactions to other people will stop and you'll begin to just observe their behavior without being affected by it.

Why is this law so important to how we create? Because until we can own all parts of ourselves—by healing and embracing those part of us we don't like and developing those parts of us we admire in others but we can't see in ourselves yet—we remain disconnected from God to a certain degree. And true prosperity hinges on our ability to consistently connect with God and how well we can receive what He has in store for us, which includes some bumpy times and some smooth sailing times.

The Law of Projection is also true for those qualities we do admire in other people. When we say, "I wish I could be like so and so…" that is also the Law of Projection playing out in your life. These are positive qualities in us that we're not developing, but we're seeing them in other people. If you see someone confidently speaking in front of others and wish you could do the same, know that you can! This is part of honoring your gifts and talents and then developing them, which always brings us closer to heaven.

And now for a little bit of honesty…

List three things that drive you crazy in other people.

1.

2.

3.

List three things you admire in others that you wish were qualities you possessed.

1.

2.

3.

Law of Compensation: You get equal returns for that which is given. In other words, you get what you give.

You'll always be compensated for your efforts and your contribution, whatever it is, however much or however little. And you can never be compensated in the long term for more than what you've put in. So, be very aware of how you're contributing to your life of prosperity, especially in your thoughts, and in your method of procedure.

What's a method of procedure? It's the angle or the way you "approach" life. I titled this book *The Prosperity Approach* for a reason: if we want prosperity, we must approach it in a completely different way from what we've known! We must change our method of procedure.

Some places where people fall short in this law are:

- expecting something for nothing
- hunting for cheap things, or refusing to buy things unless they're a bargain
- begrudging spending money

Can you see where the approach or method of procedure is dripping in scarcity? That's the scarcity approach! You're learning The Prosperity Approach, and for the Law of Compensation to work for you, you must be aware of what you're giving, because it's going to come back to you in the same way you gave it.

My son and I drove to Los Angeles, CA from Salt Lake City, UT to attend a course together. I didn't want to spend $3.03 a gallon for gas in LA, figuring for sure that it would cheaper in another city. We ended up spending an extra twenty minutes looking for a gas station in a smaller town, where it was $3.23 a gallon! In my effort to save a few dollars, I wasted a bunch of time and it ended up costing me more anyway. My method of procedure was hunting for a cheap thing, not taking the prosperity approach. It was a fabulous lesson that reminded me that as I just use the resources around me and trust, I'll be taken care of.

Does this mean you don't buy things on sale or look for discounts? Of course not! But when you trust that as you show up to play full out, the universe will conspire to help you, you'll actually find things on sale very easily, and discounts will come out of nowhere. And when they don't, you know that's all right, because eventually they will.

Law of Divine Compensation: Even when we experience diminishment within the material plane, within the level of spiritual substance, there's more than enough capacity for the Divine to compensate for any lack.

This law puts us right back to the two secrets of true prosperity: connecting and receiving. Divine Compensation helps us realize that no matter what we think we're lacking in our physical circumstances, there is always plenty to be created from the spiritual plane, and God knows exactly what to do to compensate for any lack.

In order for God to do this, we must be aligned to love and let go of fear. We do this by connecting to Him and receiving all the good He has for us even in the midst of the turbulent times. It's knowing that He has created us to be resilient, and we can choose to either bend with the wind like the willow tree, or stand rigid in the wind and snap. It is completely up to us.

I had many opportunities to practice putting the Law of Divine Compensation to the test while I rebuilt my business. Many times it was a daily, conscious reminder to let go of fear and focus on what I wanted to expand in my life. When the physical evidence piled up against me, and there was no money coming in but the bills were steady and reliable every month, I literally took it hour by hour, reminding myself that the laws work perfectly and I had to adjust my thinking to them. We were preserved in little ways and big ways, and as I stayed flexible and willing to bend, I opened up to receiving in ways I'd never done before. My family rallied around me, supporting me in every way. My children stayed healthy and free from injuries, and people came across my path to help me regain my confidence, strengthen my message and firm up my resolve to keep on keeping on.

Whatever you're going through, know that it's here because it's the next step in your spiritual growth and evolution. You're ready for it, and you can handle it! God will compensate you for any lack or loss, so long as you allow Him to. He does it in His own time and in His own way, which usually means it's going to take a bit longer than we'd like and look different from what we'd pictured. And it will be absolutely perfect!

Chapter 5
Going All Mental

———————•———————

There is no labor from which most people shrink as they do from that of sustained and consecutive thought; it is the hardest work in the world.

—Wallace Wattles

True prosperity is a process, and most of the process happens between our ears. When my kids were young we used to watch "George Shrinks" on PBS. His dad used to say, "Way to use your noggin for something more than an eyebrow holder!" And we've got to use our own brains for more than an eyebrow holder if we are going to create true prosperity.

There are four mental laws that are extremely helpful to know when working on the mental pillar of prosperity and developing a prosperity mindset. Can you handle four more laws on top of the twenty-one you just read through? I know you can!

Rule #1: The mind must think. You can guide it, but you can't stop it.

The mind is in a constant state of activity. So, in regard to the universal law of Cause & Effect, the planting process and the harvesting process are always going on. You can choose not to guide your thoughts and let them wander wherever they feel like, but that's not going to stop the harvest. What it does stop is your ability to control what's being harvested in your mind.

Rule #2: The mind thinks boundlessly

The mind is in a constant state of activity, and it's boundless in its capabilities. You have an imagination that is literally limitless. You can think of anything! Wordplay and innovation are created in the mind to help you look at things from a different perspective. You can take information and date and shape them into creative new meanings.

My ten-year-old daughter came running into the house after playing out in the field with her friend for several hours. She was sweaty and dirty and had scratches all over her arms and legs. I asked her what she had been up to and she informed me they had been building a fort. But they wanted it to be a secret fort, so they had to cover it with sticks to camouflage it. She said, "it was really sticky, Mom." I looked at her in confusion, and asked her if the trees had been covered with sap or something. She stared at me like I was not the brightest bulb in the pack. "No, Mom," she said. "There were a lot of *sticks*. It was sticky! That's why I have all these scratches on me." Her wordplay on "sticky" completely changed what I was picturing in my mind.

Wordplay is just one of the many facets of our incredible imagination. And children use their imagination correctly all the time, to create "alternate realities" of play that are expansive and fulfilling. As adults, we use our imagination to "be realistic", so we can be "prepared in case anything goes wrong." All this does is cripple our faith and keep us paralyzed in fear.

Rule #3: The mind thinks exclusively, only one thought at a time

You might be tempted to argue with me on this one, but it's true. You can only think one thought at a time. Your mind thinks so fast that sometimes it seems that you're thinking about more than one thought at a time, but that's not the case. Only one player can perform on the stage of your mind at any given time, and you have absolute control over which player that is.

But know this: any thought that becomes dominant in your mind represents *a choice*.

Rule #4: The mind drives the body

In Dennis R. Deaton's book, *The Book on Mind Management*, he makes a distinction between the mind and the brain. The mind is the spirit, and the brain is part of the body. He goes on to explain that the body is dependent on the mind. The mind wills, the brain directs, and the body enacts. The mind is independent, the brain and body are dependent. The body can affect the mind and the mind can affect the body, but the mind takes precedence. When the mind commits, the body has no choice but to respond. It may resist or complain, but in the final analysis, the mind rules.

My son went to New York City with his high school band his junior year. He doesn't like crowds and prefers to stay at home, but we thought it would be a wonderful experience for him to see a big metropolitan city and expand his horizons a bit. The thing he wanted least to do was go to the top of the Empire State Building.

I got a frantic text from him while he was on his trip saying that he was dizzy and sweaty, he felt nauseous and the room kept spinning. I told him to ask the chaperones if he could go back to the hotel and skip the evening activity, and he informed me he'd already gotten permission. When I asked him what he was missing out on, guess what he said? Yep! The Empire State Building! I have no doubt that he was dizzy and nauseated, but it wasn't because of the food he ate or being dehydrated. His mind created sickness in his body so he wouldn't have to go. He wasn't faking it, it was the power of his mind.

I experience the power of my mind every morning when I convince my body to get out of bed and work out. My brain and body love to resist and complain, but once my mind commits, away we go!

The Prosperity Mindset

Your mind is the most powerful computer in the world. And you create your reality according to the vibration of your thoughts and beliefs, your inner frequency. For most people, the programs that have been installed resonate at a vibration that is far below the frequency of prosperity, and you can tell that by looking around at your circumstances.

So, what do we get to do? Install new programs, of course! But first, let's break it down a bit so you understand what's going on behind the scenes in your miraculous mind.

First, draw a circle about the size of a grapefruit.

Next, draw a horizontal line separating the circle in half, with a top half and a bottom half. In the top half of the circle write "conscious." On the lower half of the circle write "subconscious." Draw an arrow out from the line separating the two and write "filter." You can also write its official name: Reticular Activating System or RAS, but filter also works!

Now that it's labeled, let's discuss.

Your mind has two parts to it: the conscious and the subconscious. The *conscious* mind is what makes decisions. It can create new ideas, it has the ability to accept or reject ideas, and is our *awareness*.

The *subconscious* mind is what runs all of our belief systems or programs. The party happens in the subconscious! It doesn't have the ability to reject any idea: it accepts all ideas as truth, whether or not they actually are. It runs all your automatic functions: breathing, heart beating, blinking eyes, digestion, blood flow, and so forth. Its job is to keep you alive and safe. The subconscious is the center for emotions, which is important to remember, and is also called your heart or your spirit.

There is an invisible filter between the two, which is officially called the Reticular Activating System, or RAS. The filter distinguishes between truth and lies and allows your conscious mind to kick ideas out if it determines they're not useful. I also like to call it the "bouncer." It can bounce ideas out if they're not useful to our vision of prosperity. Our filter isn't fully in place until we're about eight years old. That's why children believe everything you tell them. It's accepted by the subconscious without question, and those programs come back to haunt us as we get older and want to create prosperity.

Note: Ideas and beliefs will stay in the subconscious mind *until another belief takes it over.*

Would you like an example?

Your conscious mind might think that having money is a good thing, but most of us have subconscious programming that doesn't agree with that. So, if we say wealth affirmations, we usually feel like we're lying, or we feel guilty for wanting money. It also makes us sabotage ourselves anytime we set a new money goal or are close to achieving that money goal. We'll flub up interviews, not even apply for promotions or jobs, even give money away or spend it on frivolous things, all in an effort to get it out of our experience.

Marilyn Jenett says in her book *Feel Free to Prosper,* "In order to manifest our desire, the conscious and subconscious minds must *agree* on the idea."

In order to do this, we must influence the subconscious mind. That means those new thoughts you can think in your conscious mind, about prosperity and your ability to build it, must pass through the filter into your subconscious mind. Because that's what runs the show!

However, our subconscious is quite crafty. After all, its job is to keep you alive and safe, and so far, so good! No matter how miserable you've been, you're still alive, right? The subconscious doesn't want to change *any* aspect of that. It has no idea how safe you'll be if you live the life of your dreams, because you've never done it before! So, we've got to be crafty in influencing the subconscious. We've got to be subtle and use what Marilyn calls, "friendly persuasion."

In order for the new belief or idea about life to be able to pass through the filter, you must allow it to remain as a *dominant thought* in your conscious mind **until it's accepted on an emotional level**.

It's important to know that there are two factors that determine programs that run in subconscious:

1. Repetitive thoughts
2. Thoughts that are charged with emotion

Emotions are what put new programming into the subconscious mind.

"Man becomes what he thinks about all day long."—*Ralph Waldo Emerson*

Your prosperity is directly proportional to the intensity of your emotions surrounding it. Remember, the subconscious is the center for your emotions. So they play a starring role in your prosperous life.

Emotions are part of you, though you are not your emotions. You are above them, because emotions are effects, not causes! Every single emotion can be traced back to a thought.

I remember sitting in my office one day, feeling discouraged and depressed. But remembering that emotions are effects, I started tracing the emotion back to what I had been thinking about. I'd been thinking about how hard life felt, how nothing was working, and how I wanted to give up! And the scary part is I wasn't even consciously aware that I was thinking such negative thoughts until I traced them from my emotions. No wonder I felt discouraged and depressed! But the thoughts didn't come because of the emotions. The emotions came directly from my thoughts.

Thoughts cause emotions. Emotions do not cause thoughts.

Write the above two sentences down three times, and say it out loud!

1.

2.

3.

Emotions are powerful indicators of where you're vibrating at any given moment. Use them the way they were intended: to keep you consciously aware of your inner frequency, and to shift it up when necessary.

If we want different results, we must change the cause.

Emotions can be tricky little things, though. Have you ever had a hard time "feeling" excited about your dream, especially because it seems so far away? I know this was a real stumbling block for me for a very long time.

Any time I'd say an affirmation or try to visualize the future of my dreams, I'd think to myself, "Ugh, now it's time to conjure up some enthusiasm and picture myself there."

Sound familiar? If that's you right now, take heart! Remember, one of the factors is repeating thoughts often, or using repetition. Start there! It will take longer to reach your subconscious because it has to be accepted emotionally before it's lodged in your subconscious, but what is a belief? A belief is just a thought we've thought so many times we accept it as the truth. Say a thought often enough and eventually you'll believe it's true. It's even okay if you feel like you're lying to yourself at first! It's all right; our minds lie to us all day long. We make up stories about things that just aren't true all the time. And usually those stories don't support us in going after our dreams. So, as Leslie Householder likes to say, "If you're going to lie to yourself anyway, you might as well lie constructively!"

If you want different results, you must change the cause. Thoughts that are repeated often and that are charged with emotion control your results. So, instead of working more hours or getting yet another part-time job, get to work on your mind and watch things change!

Honesty check:

How much thought are you giving your current circumstances? Are those thoughts positive or negative? How much emotion accompany those thoughts? What are the emotions that follow your dominant thoughts about your current circumstances? Jot it down here.

_____

_____

_____

_____

_____

See if this silent conversation sounds familiar to you:

"Oh crap! I forgot that bill was coming out of the account today. And now I'm overdrawn . . again. Of course! Why is this always happening to me? And now I have to pay more money that I DON'T have? I am SO TIRED of being broke all the time! This is such a hassle! I am DONE living life this way! I DON'T want this to happen again! I WISH I wasn't poor!"

I can't tell you how many times I had monologues in my mind when that would happen. My stomach would drop to my knees, I'd be filled with resentment toward everyone! But when you do that, this what you're effectively saying to your subconscious and the universe: This is the way I want my life to be because I am *so* passionate about it.

Why is that? You're declaring what you don't want! You're being very clear about what you want to have stopped. However, your subconscious and the universe don't recognize or understand words of negation like don't, wish it wasn't, etc. All your subconscious knows is that you've thought this thought a lot, and it is supercharged with emotion, so it takes it as an instruction and moves to fulfill it.

So, to change it…

Get passionate about what you want! Picture what you want. And deal with the unpleasant things in your current circumstances with the least amount of emotion possible. They still need to be dealt with. I don't recommend hiding the utility bill and pretending it never came. If you can't pay it, call them up and tell them you can't and ask them to work with you. Stay in your integrity, but deal with it in a matter-of-fact way, rather than getting upset by it.

How to reprogram your subconscious, but done in game form!

When you find yourself spinning in dark emotions, it's crucial to pivot out of that as quickly as possible. We've got to get you on the same frequency as your dream if you're going to get your dream. And we've got to do it often, which means we get to practice! But I also know how compelling that physical evidence can be, and that sometimes we'll get caught up in the emotion of it all. When that happens, play the Pivot game.

When you're experiencing drama, you're in your story. We give meaning to everything that happens to us. Most of the time that meaning is not supportive of what we want. Playing the Pivot game is essential when you're in your story, and that is also the hardest time to do it. But I know you can!

Here's how it works. Whenever you're feeling a negative emotion, get into conscious awareness of it, but from an angle of curiosity. You can say to yourself, "Hmm…this came up for a reason, and this is very interesting. What is it I want?" After answering that question, simply turn your attention to what it is you want. Your mind will tempt you to replay the situation that caused the negative emotion, but hold firm and simply ask yourself again what you want. Pivot toward the feeling you want to feel, and choose the thoughts that support that feeling. The moment you stop putting attention on the negative emotion, it stops the attraction of that emotion, and begins the attraction of a positive emotion. Keep pivoting to the positive emotion. Refuse to dive back down the rabbit hole of negativity. You'll find yourself circling around it, for sure, but do not look in it or go down it!

Don't talk to anyone else about the negative situation, because this pivots your attention back on what you don't want, and pumps more energy to it. That will be the hardest thing to do—not recruiting others to be on your side. But stay diligent and before too long you'll find that you've pivoted far enough into a positive emotion that you can look at the situation without anything other than objective curiosity. And then you can solve the problem from there, if it still needs to be solved.

This will take some practice. Depending on how caught up you get in your story, at first you might find yourself spending a lot of time trying to pivot from something. It's well worth the effort, though! Allow me to illustrate what this looked like for me:

I once got an email from a client who wanted to terminate her contract. Her email was filled with accusations that were unfounded, untrue, and surprisingly hurtful to me. I found myself immediately get defensive and want to respond in kind. This was the perfect opportunity to pivot!

The first thing I did was close out the email and physically walk out of my office to put some distance between myself and the situation. (pivot) I wanted nothing more than to text my husband what had happened, but I didn't. (pivot) My next thought was to call a colleague and tell her all about it, but again, I didn't. (pivot) Instead, I asked myself what I wanted to feel, and commanded myself to follow that thought. (pivot) I thought about what needed to be done that day (pivot) and made plans for the next thing on my list. I refused to give the situation any energy by thinking about it (pivot), even though that's the only thing I wanted to focus on. I distracted my mind with uplifting music (pivot) and forced myself to focus on something else (pivot). I remember commanding myself to pivot away from the negativity. In my mind I saw that giant, black rabbit hole, and I was circling around it, debating whether or not to jump down into it. I kept asking myself what I wanted to feel instead, and shifted the energy into the better feeling thought.

It took about an hour, but I successfully managed to pivot away from that situation and have a productive day. It was several hours later, after checking in on my emotions around the situation and discovering that they were more neutral than charged, that I allowed myself to answer her email. And it was respectful, professional and detached. The situation resolved itself without further drama.

That's the power of pivoting. Notice that I didn't go into denial about it and tell myself to just forget about it, nor did I reflexively dive headlong into it. In the moment of drama I had to *pivot from it* so I could disconnect from the negative emotion it caused. Then later, after I'd connected to a positive thought and there was no more charge (or virtually no charge) in my emotions concerning the issue, I allowed myself back into the situation where I could be emotionally detached and handle everything quickly from there.

As you practice, you'll actually *feel* the shift in your mind and your body as you go from tense, uptight and triggered to calm, collected and neutral. It's a very powerful experience, and entirely within *your* control.

Five words that will change your life

Before we close out this chapter, I want to share with you the five words that will change your life, because they will instantly begin changing your subconscious programs in a way that's really easy to feel emotional about. These words incorporate visualization with emotion, which are the two ingredients necessary for manifestation.

"Wouldn't it be nice if. . ."

Why is this question so powerful? Because it instantly gets the conscious and subconscious to agree, which is one of the rules to subconscious reprogramming! Saying an affirmation like, "I am wealthy," immediately starts an argument in your mind, doesn't it? But to say, "Wouldn't it be nice if I were wealthy?" immediately gets your two minds in agreement. They'll say, "Yeah! It would be awesome!"

Next, take it a step further and ask yourself, "Okay, what would it look like if I was wealthy? What would I do with my day? Where would

I work? What would I eat? Where would I live? Wow, wouldn't that be nice?"

Then ask yourself, "How would it feel if I were wealthy? What would that feel like? I'd feel fulfilled, I'd feel victorious. I'd feel a huge sense of accomplishment at what I'd achieved, and I'd feel completely successful!" Notice I didn't say, "I'd feel awesome." And leave it at that. Use words that convey emotion, not just adjectives.

A word of caution before leaving this chapter:

Do not be deceived by the simplicity of these two techniques. They're simple by design, so that you'll do them. But many times we'll sabotage ourselves by saying, "Oh, that's all it is? That's so simple . . . I'll do it later." And then we never do it. So, to jump start you on the "Wouldn't it be nice . . ." game, try playing it right now.

> *"When the solution is simple, God is answering." --Einstein*

Wouldn't it be nice if...

_____

_____

_____

Wow! What would that look like?

_____

_____

_____

Ooh! What do you think it will feel like?

_____

_____

_____

See? Isn't that easy? And fun! I play this game several times every day. I play it in the shower, when I'm getting ready in the morning, when I'm driving in the car or waiting in traffic. We even play it as a family around the dinner table every night! This game right here has the power to change every part of your life. So play it!

Chapter 6
Physical: The Third Pillar of Prosperity

———————•———————

The things that we love tell us what we are.
–Thomas Aquinas

Prosperity isn't created in isolation. If we were meant to do it alone, we'd all have our very own planets where we would be the only people on it and we'd be happy. But that's not how it works.

I had a business coach once who continually told her clients, "Connection is currency." I was uncomfortable with that idea, because at that time my belief was that if I was connecting with people just to make money, it felt insincere and manipulative to me. I didn't like the idea of, "What can I get from that person?" So I shied away from that idea for several years.

However, as I've come to learn about how true prosperity is created, I've realized that my coach was exactly right. Relationship currency, when used correctly, oftentimes turns into financial currency, where it's a win-win for everyone involved.

For high levels of prosperity to occur, authentically connecting with other people is critical.

Authentically connecting with others can be difficult to do, especially when we've got different backgrounds and personalities, and things that are important to others just don't make a difference to us. Have you ever met someone that you immediately click with? Of course! Have you ever met someone that immediate repels you? Of course! Do you wonder why? It's because you're "coded" differently.

My friend Cheri Tree created a real-world methodology called B.A.N.K. ™ to authentically connect with others and boost her bottom line. She started her career in the financial planning industry, and her first year she made $700. Knowing there was no way she could ever survive on that, over the next five years Cheri took every sales training she could get her hands on. And within five years she had increased her sales from $700 a year to $72,000. By most standards, she was considered successful. But she knew a key component was missing. There was something about the way she was connecting with some people but not connecting with others that nagged at her. So she set off on a quest to find out what that was. Though she created B.A.N.K. initially to increase her sales, she found that it also added enormous prosperity to her relationships.

What is B.A.N.K.?

B.A.N.K. is a proven method of communication backed by over 2500 years of personality science that teaches you to crack someone's personality code in 90 seconds or less. Why would you want to do this? Because by cracking someone's code you automatically create deeper levels of connection and understanding, called relationship currency, which very naturally increases financial prosperity. When you can crack someone's code, you can see what's important to the other person and then genuinely serve their needs, because it's based on what's important to them, not you. When people know you, like you, and trust you, they feel a connection with you, and they want to do business with you.

What do I mean by cracking their code? Take a look at the picture below.

This is called a Cryptex. It's a portable device designed to hide secret messages. Cryptex is a combination of two words: Cryptology—the science of locking up secret information, and Codex—the written scripture or paper rolled up and locked inside this device. It was made famous in Dan Brown's book *The DaVinci Code*. In the book, what was locked inside this device was the secret to the holy grail. The only way to access it was to crack the code.

But this device was booby trapped. The secret was wrapped around a vial of vinegar, and if you put in the wrong code the vial was designed to break and the vinegar would dissolve the scroll and the secret written on it. And you would be left with what?

Absolutely nothing!

So, what does this have to do with personality science and cracking people's personality code? Realize that everyone you talk to has an invisible Cryptex of their own. And each one has a little rolled up piece of paper inside that Cryptex with the word "yes" written on it. Whatever the question is, the answer is yes. How helpful would it be to know what the code is in order to crack it and get to the yes?

How many times have you accidently broken the vial of vinegar and watched your yes dissolve into a no in front of your eyes? And you're like, what happened? Come back! Have you ever had a conversation with someone that started off well but then suddenly you were in a fight? And you're wondering where it veered off. It's because you cracked their vial of vinegar, or your own vial of vinegar was cracked, and the "yes" dissolved, the connection was broken, and the conversation was pretty much over.

So, the real question is, how many times is this happening to you and how much is it costing you in your relationships and in money? It's cost me a ton in both over the years.

The science of B.A.N.K. is the concept of the four personality types that was invented 2,500 years ago by Hippocrates, the father of medicine. He made the theory famous when he realized he could divide the entire human race into four parts based on the main personality types. He called it *The Theory of the Four Temperaments.* It was proven so well, scientifically, that he could actually diagnose his medical patients differently based on one of the four personality types.

What Cheri realized was that *she* was one of those four types and more than likely, just like everyone else, every time she talked to someone, she was coming from *her own point of view.* By doing that she was only connecting with and speaking to the one personality type that matched hers. That meant she was disconnecting from the other three personality types! She left a ton of money on the table doing that.

Have you ever had a co-worker or a child you couldn't connect with? It's because you're speaking from different points of view, in different languages. That's all.

Once Cheri realized that she was dealing with different personality types, she began to wonder if people made buying decisions based on their personalities as well. So she began to study them. Before long she realized that yes, people make all of their decisions based on their personalities and their values. All she needed to do was find what drove a person, what was important to them on the level of their *values*, and talk to them in the language they can understand. When she did that, her sales went from $72,000 one year to $500,000 the next! (If you're a numbers person, that's a 695% increase in one year.) Over the next three years she hit $1,000,000 and is now a millionaire several times over. She has since written a book called *Why They Buy*, which details her journey and philosophy about B.A.N.K.

If you've ever taken a personality assessment before (and I know you have, because what's the most fascinating subject to you? Yourself!), you might be wondering how B.A.N.K. compares to other personality assessments. B.A.N.K. is exactly the same, only completely different from every other assessment in the world. Why? Because unlike every other assessment, it's not psychology based. It is *values* based. And when you know what someone else values you can influence them in a way that is genuine, authentic, and creates a win-win for everyone. Knowing what *my* personality type is doesn't make me relate to you better. But knowing what drives and motivates *you* definitely helps me relate to you better!

I learned this when raising my children. They're motivated by completely different things. One child just wants to make sure everyone else is taken care of. The other child gets bored easily and just wants to have fun. One of my children stresses out if we're going to be late to anything. Another one often wanders off into daydreams in the middle of dinner. Gender and age have nothing to do with it. It has everything to do with how those kids are coded, and the personality that was wired into them.

What B.A.N.K. stands for

B.A.N.K., of course, is an acronym. To illustrate this acronym, we'll use an analogy of a box to describe what each personality type is like.

B stands for *Blueprint.* This person lives **inside the box.** They believe, "If you're early you're on time, if you're on time you're late, if you're late you're fired."

A stands for *Action.* This personality type lives **outside the box**. Action personality types think, "Rules were made to be broken!"

N stands for *Nurturing.* The person with this personality would **recycle the box**. Nurturing personality types say, "Why can't we all just get along?"

K stands for *Knowledge.* This person **engineers the box**! And Knowledge types think, "Beam me up, Scotty. There's no intelligent life down here."

The really cool thing about B.A.N.K. is that we all have every part of the code wired into us. Why is that such a big deal? Because even if someone else's code is not our dominant code, once we understand and recognize the clues that the other person puts out concerning their code, we can easily step into *that* part of our code and see the world *through the other person's lenses.*

We reveal our B.A.N.K. code in practically every part of our lives: from the kind of job we have, to the clothes we wear, the kind of homes we live in, the cars we drive, the vacations we take, down to the books we read and what we do for fun. When you learn how to crack that code, the world opens up for you in ways you can't imagine!

B.A.N.K. closes the gap, which helps you connect deeply, authentically, and influence others in a way that feels honest and genuine. And whether you're trying to influence a new client, or influence your boss into giving you a raise, or get a new job, convince your spouse to do the remodel or take that vacation you've always wanted, or even asking someone out on a date, knowing B.A.N.K. will give you the edge you need to influence others and create transactions where everybody wins.

B.A.N.K. has the power to change your life

When I first learned B.A.N.K., I immediately wanted to crack my code. I'm sure you'll want to crack yours, too. No worries; I'll show you how to do it shortly. My B.A.N.K. code is NBAK—Nurturing, Blueprint, Action, then Knowledge. And Knowledge is by far the lowest part of my code. Once I learned how to crack my code, of course I wanted to crack my family's code!

At the time I had a sixteen-year-old son I struggled to connect with for many years. I knew that part of the estrangement was that he was a sixteen-year-old boy, with lots of raging hormones going on. But when I got really honest, I hadn't been able to relate to him since he learned how to talk. He was different from me in every single aspect. The more I tried to love him, the faster and more fully he pulled away from me. It had gotten to the point where, no matter what I asked him, he answered with a grunt or one word. He wouldn't look me in the eye, and whenever I tried to hug him he'd stiffen up, keeping his arms firmly at his side.

I knew he'd crack his code, though. No one can resist wanting to learn more about themselves! Can you guess what his code was? K.B.A.N. His dominant code was my lowest code. And *my* dominant code was *his* lowest code! Eureka! We'd found the answer to why he continually pulled away from me: I wasn't speaking his code! I kept breaking the vial of vinegar whenever I tried to connect. And since I had taken the B.A.N.K. training, all I had to do was immerse myself in what makes a Knowledge personality tick, and then speak to him in his language.

Within five days, not weeks—days, my son had completely turned around! I watched him blossom in front of my eyes. Suddenly he was responding to me and relating to me, because I was honoring his personality code. I was speaking **his** language.

Learning B.A.N.K. has done more to repair relationships in my family than anything else I've ever experienced. What's even better, as he saw me honoring his code, he very naturally started honoring mine. We're at the point now where he'll seek me out just to give me a hug, because Nurturing personality types like hugs a lot. What's so significant about that? Knowledge types aren't so big on physical touch or being outwardly expressive with their emotions all the time. So the fact that he's also speaking my code has done wonders for our relationship.

Both of my parents are very strong Blueprints. Remember the mantra of the Blueprint? Time is very valuable to them; they don't like it wasted. Christmas dinner at their house always starts at 4:00 p.m. One year my family walked in at 4:03. The prayer had been said, the line was formed, and some people were already eating! I remember looking at my watch and wondering if we were really late, if we had gotten the time wrong, or what. Nope; we were just three minutes late.

Before I'd learned B.A.N.K. my feelings would have been deeply hurt by them not waiting a lousy three minutes for us to get there. But since I knew that they were strong Blueprints, and true Blueprints live and die by their clocks, I wasn't offended at all. In fact, it was really quite funny, and just so telling about how they're wired. I didn't look at them with anything but compassion and love.

By the way, we learned our lesson. We meet them for a fun family dinner out once a month now. My husband (who is also a strong Blueprint) will remind me to text them if we're going to be more than one minute late so that they're not annoyed. I forgot to text them once; I got a text one minute after our arranged time asking where we were and how far out we'd be. I just shook my head and smiled.

Ready to crack your code?

Would you like to know what your B.A.N.K. code is? Here's a fast and free way you can crack it: go to http://mybankcode.com/prosperity and crack your code. You can also access a free assessment at http://mybankcode.com. It will require the access code *prosperity*. It's a ton of fun, takes under two minutes, and you can even send the link along to family and friends so they can crack their own codes. Once you've cracked your code, a report will be emailed to you that explains more about each of the codes so you can learn more about you and everyone else around you.

Chapter 7
The Prosperity Approach Recap

———————•———————

Simplicity is the ultimate sophistication.
–DaVinci

Well, there you have it. Your 3-2-1- Formula to create massive prosperity. To sum it all up, here it is in a nutshell:

3 Pillars energetic, mental and physical **+ 2 Secrets** Connecting with God and Receiving **= 1 Prosperous Life** a level of living not governed by fear or lack

It's simple, isn't it? Of course, simple doesn't mean easy. But it also doesn't mean complicated. Creating the level of prosperity you long for takes awareness, mental discipline and tenacity. Start on your prosperity journey and continually refer back to this book as your prosperity handbook. Time will pass whether you're on a prosperity journey or a scarcity journey. But when you choose the prosperity approach, you'll be so busy being in awareness and deliberate thinking, and you'll be having so much fun cracking people's codes and connecting with them, that you'll soon begin to realize that the journey is the destination. You'll more easily feel happy, relieved and supported, and you'll feel that more and more often. Your confidence will grow, and your faith and trust in God will explode. The money will come, because money is a byproduct of your thoughts and beliefs. Prosperity is guaranteed as you continually apply the formula.

You might feel like you've scratched the surface of prosperity, though. If that's how you feel, you would be right! The techniques and tools included in this workbook have the power to change your life. But it's kind of like scratching your own back—you can only reach so far until you need someone else to hit the spots you can't quite get to.

To assist with this, you can download a free gift I created to help you get started today. This is a wonderful resource to help you get going, with practical, easily implemented exercises to clear fears and money blocks and literally align you with prosperity. Download your copy at **http://prosperityapproach.com/freegift**

I love to hear from my tribe! If you have questions or comments you can connect with me via facebook at http://facebook.com/simplyallyson

Or email me at allyson@allysonchavez.com

So, what do I do next?

I've included a quick guide to assist you in consistently applying the prosperity formula while avoiding overwhelm. And you can do this in nine simple steps!

1. Determine which ways you best connect to your Higher Power. Commit to doing at least one of those things every day so you continually reconnect throughout the day.

2. Pick three ways that are easiest for you to receive. Practice at least one of them every day.

3. Practice muscle testing on your beliefs and where your inner frequency is. Feel your trust and confidence grow!

4. Pay strict attention to your emotions, because they lead directly to your thoughts and tell you where you're vibrating at any given moment.

5. Pick one law to focus on and see how it shows up in your life. You can do this daily, or even spend a few days or a week on one law at a time. If you're not sure which law to pick, choose the one that jumps out at you. Or muscle test for it.

6. When it feels like nothing is working, use one of the laws to pull you through that time more quickly and smoothly.

7. Begin reprogramming your subconscious for prosperity by playing the "Wouldn't it be Nice" game several times every day.

8. If you feel yourself being swept up in negative emotions, shift out of those lower frequencies by playing "What's working for me now?"

9. Refer often to the report you got after cracking your code. Observe those around you—how they dress, where they work, the kind of car they drive, what they talk about for fun—and see if you can crack their codes!

Chapter 8
Join The Prosperity Revolution!

———————•———————

The Prosperity Approach is a process that you apply every day. As you consciously focus on prosperity using the methods taught in this book, it will eventually sink into your subconscious and become second nature. But if you'd like to fast track your results, **you must surround yourself with the frequency of prosperity**. Getting to that higher frequency and maintaining it can be pretty difficult to do on your own. Of course, you already know that. If you could consistently hold that higher frequency, you wouldn't have read this book!

To supercharge your results, and keep you in this powerful conversation, I've created several programs to fit every budget as you master The Prosperity Approach.

If you'd like to stay in this prosperity conversation, add more prosperity tools to your toolbox, and be supported by a like-minded community, I invite you to join the Prosperity Revolution. This is an ongoing monthly online program to help anchor in prosperity through different techniques and exercises that you'll learn on a weekly basis.

Each week you'll receive (via a Facebook Post in the secret, closed group):

--A 10 minute (ish) audio or video training on one of the cornerstones of prosperity (spiritual, energetic, mental, physical)

You'll also get:

--Ongoing contact with Allyson and other like-minded, high thinking people

--1 live 60 minute (ish) Zoom group chat with Allyson every month to ask questions, get more group energy work done, and stay connected to the frequency of prosperity

--Plus, we'll be doing experiments, playing with energy and connecting you with **the power you have to create whatever reality you desire.**

Can you say FUN??!!

Everything is recorded to give you maximum freedom and flexibility, and with just one call a month, it doesn't require a big time commitment. This is an ongoing program, with no contracts. You can cancel anytime and join anytime! And it's only $30 a month, after a 7 day FREE trial!

How do I sign up?

To sign up go **to http://prosperityapproach.com/revolution**. Type in your credit card and billing info. You'll then be added to The Prosperity Revolution secret, closed Facebook group.

You'll get 7 days free! After that your card will automatically be charged $30 a month.

If at any time you want to cancel, simply shoot an email to allyson@allysonchavez.com and put 'cancel my subscription' in the subject line, and we'll do it with no questions asked.

Come play with me in my prosperity playground. **Invite your friends to join you there as well**. You're on the right track--now let's get you running that track!

Money Secrets: 30 Day Challenge

This online program has everything you need to create different results with money. Every day for thirty days you'll receive specific instructions, education and techniques about how to change your experience with money. These are the exact approaches I used to change everything around money. You'll get a 60 minute energy session, meditations, tracking sheets and an accountability calendar to assist you through the month. Each technique can be done pretty much anywhere and takes five minutes or less to complete.

This robust program has previously sold for $297, but when you invest in yourself you'll spend a fraction of that amount. It's only $37 when you access it at http://moneysecrets101.com/start

The Prosperity Approach Live: 3 Day Intensive

Immerse yourself in the behind the scenes mechanics of prosperity. I continually tell my clients, "You must know what you're doing and why you're doing it." This live intensive teaches you the *hows* and *whys* of creating results that matter in your business, relationships and life. We'll dive deep into each of the pillars of prosperity and spend a full day on each one. I'll teach you the method I developed to move energy quickly, and you'll leave the first day knowing how to remove energetic, emotional and money blocks from you, your family and your friends.

You'll also learn specific, fast techniques to get into the subconscious and change the programs that are running there. The party happens in the subconscious, so this day will be packed with fun "party games" to end procrastination, ramp up your commitment and easily create the results that matter in every area of your life.

As if that weren't enough to completely change your life, you'll get hands-on training and certification in BANK fundamentals. You'll leave knowing how to crack other people's codes and talk to them in a way that creates prosperity for everyone.

It's three days. Three life skills. An incredibly powerful conversation all about the *hows* to changing your life. For more information go to http://prosperityapproach.com/3dayintensive

Prosperity Essentials Online Course

If you're looking for more hands-on guidance to create ultimate, lasting prosperity, the Prosperity Essentials Online Course is a great fit for you. This three month online course, taught live by Allyson, dives deeper into The Prosperity Formula. Included in this course is a workbook, access to Allyson via the secret, closed Facebook group as well as an app called Voxer, weekly live, interactive training calls that are recorded and available for download, and the support of a like-minded community. Go to http://prosperityapproach.com/course for more information.

Private VIP Mentoring

If you're looking to customize your prosperity experience, Allyson offers private mentoring by application only. Visit http://allysonchavez.com and click on the 'are you ready?' tab in the bottom RH corner to access and fill out an application.

Allyson shares her Ultimate Prosperity message on international stages and would love to speak to your group! Email her at allyson@allysonchavez.com for events, a media kit and her speaking schedule.

Made in the USA
Middletown, DE
03 September 2021